READINGS ON

SOPHOCLES

Other titles in the Greenhaven Press Literary Companion Series:

American Authors

Nathaniel Hawthorne
Ernest Hemingway
Arthur Miller
Herman Melville
John Steinbeck
Mark Twain

British Authors

Jane Austen

British Literature

The Canterbury Tales
Shakespeare: The Comedies
Shakespeare: The Sonnets
Shakespeare: The Tragedies

THE GREENHAVEN PRESS
Literary Companion
TO WORLD AUTHORS

READINGS ON

SOPHOCLES

David Bender, *Publisher*
Bruno Leone, *Executive Editor*
Scott Barbour, *Managing Editor*
Bonnie Szumski, *Series Editor*
Don Nardo, *Book Editor*

Greenhaven Press, San Diego, CA

Library of Congress Cataloging-in-Publication Data

Readings on Sophocles / Don Nardo, book editor.
    p.   cm. — (The Greenhaven Press literary companion to world authors)
   Includes bibliographical references and index.
   ISBN 1-56510-581-8 (pbk. : alk. paper). —
ISBN 1-56510-582-6 (lib. : alk. paper)
   1. Sophocles—Criticism and interpretation. 2. Greek drama (Tragedy)—History and criticism. 3. Mythology, Greek, in literature. I. Nardo, Don, 1947– . II. Series.
PA4417.R38   1997
882'.01–dc20   96-18327
                                                       CIP

PA
4417
.R38
1997

Cover photo: UPI/Bettmann

Copyright ©1997 by Greenhaven Press, Inc.
PO Box 289009
San Diego, CA 92198-9009
Printed in the U.S.A.

> *Wonders there are many, but*
> *none more wonderful than*
> *human beings. . . .*
> *Speech and wind-swift thought,*
> *and all the moods that create*
> *a community,*
> *They have taught themselves. . . .*
> *Cunning beyond the wildest of*
> *dreams is the skill that leads*
> *them,*
> *Sometimes to evil, other times*
> *to good.*
> *As long as they honor the laws*
> *of the land, and revere the*
> *justice of the gods,*
> *Proudly their community shall*
> *stand.*

—Sophocles,
Antigone

CONTENTS

The unseen but powerful hand of fate is an important element in ancient Greek tragedy. Yet in Sophocles' plays, says a distinguished scholar, humans are not mere playthings of the gods. Sophoclean mortals make their own choices and when these choices go against the rules set down by the gods, the mortals must pay the price.

Chapter Two: *Oedipus the King*

Chapter Three: Producing Sophocles' Plays

FOREWORD

> *"'Tis the good reader that*
> *makes the good book."*
>
> Ralph Waldo Emerson

The story's bare facts are simple: The captain, an old and scarred seafarer, walks with a peg leg made of whale ivory. He relentlessly drives his crew to hunt the world's oceans for the great white whale that crippled him. After a long search, the ship encounters the whale and a fierce battle ensues. Finally the captain drives his harpoon into the whale, but the harpoon line catches the captain about the neck and drags him to his death.

A simple story, a straightforward plot—yet, since the 1851 publication of Herman Melville's *Moby-Dick*, readers and critics have found many meanings in the struggle between Captain Ahab and the whale. To some, the novel is a cautionary tale that depicts how Ahab's obsession with revenge leads to his insanity and death. Others believe that the whale represents the unknowable secrets of the universe and that Ahab is a tragic hero who dares to challenge fate by attempting to discover this knowledge. Perhaps Melville intended Ahab as a criticism of Americans' tendency to become involved in well-intentioned but irrational causes. Or did Melville model Ahab after himself, letting his fictional character express his anger at what he perceived as a cruel and distant god?

Although literary critics disagree over the meaning of *Moby-Dick*, readers do not need to choose one particular interpretation in order to gain an understanding of Melville's novel. Instead, by examining various analyses, they can gain numerous insights into the issues that lie under the surface of the basic plot. Studying the writings of literary critics can also aid readers in making their own assessments of *Moby-Dick* and other literary works and in developing analytical thinking skills.

The Greenhaven Literary Companion Series was created with these goals in mind. Designed for young adults, this unique anthology series provides an engaging and comprehensive introduction to literary analysis and criticism. The essays included in the Literary Companion Series are chosen for their accessibility to a young adult audience and are expertly edited in consideration of both the reading and comprehension levels of this audience. In addition, each essay is introduced by a concise summation that presents the contributing writer's main themes and insights. Every anthology in the Literary Companion Series contains a varied selection of critical essays that cover a wide time span and express diverse views. Wherever possible, primary sources are represented through excerpts from authors' notebooks, letters, and journals and through contemporary criticism.

Each title in the Literary Companion Series pays careful consideration to the historical context of the particular author or literary work. In-depth biographies and detailed chronologies reveal important aspects of authors' lives and emphasize the historical events and social milieu that influenced their writings. To facilitate further research, every anthology includes primary and secondary source bibliographies of articles and/or books selected for their suitability for young adults. These engaging features make the Greenhaven Literary Companion series ideal for introducing students to literary analysis in the classroom or as a library resource for young adults researching the world's great authors and literature.

Exceptional in its focus on young adults, the Greenhaven Literary Companion Series strives to present literary criticism in a compelling and accessible format. Every title in the series is intended to spark readers' interest in leading American and world authors, to help them broaden their understanding of literature, and to encourage them to formulate their own analyses of the literary works that they read. It is the editors' hope that young adult readers will find these anthologies to be true companions in their study of literature.

INTRODUCTION

The articles, essays, and reviews selected for the Greenhaven Literary Companion to the works of Sophocles provide teachers and students with a wide range of information and opinion about the playwright and his works. The selections are divided into three broad groupings. Chapter 1 includes selections discussing Sophocles as a dramatist, including insights about and criticisms of his writing style, literary devices, and dramatic technique. One essay, for instance, explains how he, like his colleagues in Greek theater, used well-known myths as a basis for the plots and themes of his plays; other essays discuss how he used theatrical devices such as the chorus and the then unusual "third actor" to move his plots along and also to add color and complexity.

The second chapter includes selections that examine Sophocles' universally recognized masterpiece, *Oedipus the King*. Undoubtedly, a great deal more has been written about this play in the twenty-four centuries since its premiere than about the author himself. The selections range from a detailed and readable overview of the original Oedipus legend by a renowned classical scholar to a commentary on the so-called Oedipus complex and famous psychiatrist Sigmund Freud's use of Sophocles' play as inspiration for a theory that profoundly influenced the modern field of psychiatry.

Chapter 3 includes selections that discuss other plays by Sophocles as well as various attempts to translate his plays into other mediums besides theater. One essay, for example, examines the *Ajax*, focusing on the title character's strength and stubborn independence. And two reviews discuss adaptations of Sophoclean plays into black gospel music and dramatic motion pictures, respectively.

Most of the authors of the selections in this collection are late-twentieth-century writers, partly because the second half of the century witnessed a marked upsurge both in productions of Sophocles' plays on stage and film and in studies and criticisms of these works in colleges and scholarly literature. However, a few selections by respected and influential authors of earlier eras are included to show how opinions have changed and evolved over the years.

This companion to Sophocles has several special features. Most of the articles and essays explain a single, focused topic, usually a specific technique or theme Sophocles employed. The introduction to each essay summarizes the main points so that the reader knows what to expect. And interspersed within the selections the reader will find inserts that add authenticity, supplementary information, or excerpts from specific scenes discussed in the selections. Most examples of the latter are taken from famous, widely performed, and widely studied translations of Sophocles' plays. Finally, two lengthy appendixes are provided, one on the origins of theater and the other on Greek theatrical production. Both provide readers with valuable background information and a fuller context for understanding the innovative times and artistic atmosphere in which Sophocles lived and worked. Both appendixes are liberally supported by the commentary of respected modern theater historians.

SOPHOCLES: A BIOGRAPHY

Sophocles ranks as one of the three great ancient dramatists, along with his Greek colleagues Aeschylus, his senior, and Euripides, his junior. These three playwrights, all from a single city in the same era—Athens in the fifth century B.C.—are universally recognized, along with Shakespeare, as the undisputed masters of theatrical tragedy. This ranking of Sophocles, along with the fact that his works have been repeatedly performed century after century and remain the subjects of numerous stage and film productions, is a tribute to his timeless artistic genius and matchless writing skill.

Sophocles' enormous literary stature seems all the more impressive when one considers that his reputation is based on only a tiny portion of his vast artistic output. Of the 123 plays attributed to him by various ancient sources, only 7 have survived complete. Yet many literary critics and scholars consider all of these masterpieces and one—*Oedipus the King*, also frequently referred to as *Oedipus Rex* and *Oedipus Tyrannus*—as the greatest tragedy ever written. It was from this morbid but compelling tale of a man who unknowingly murders his father and then marries his mother that the modern psychoanalyst Sigmund Freud derived his idea of the Oedipus complex, which profoundly influenced the theory and practice of psychiatry in the twentieth century. Considering the huge literary and social influence of this single play, one cannot help but wonder how much greater the playwright's impact might have been had all of his works survived the ravages of time.

Unfortunately, surviving documents recording the details of Sophocles' theatrical career and personal life are also scanty, and most of these were written long after his death. The most important source is an anonymous biography, *Sophocles' Life and Works*, usually referred to simply as the *Life*, discovered in a thirteenth-century collection of his plays. When the *Life* was actually written is unknown, but it mentions several earlier biographers and paraphrases sections of their works, all of which are lost. Among them was Satyrus, a Greek who wrote a biography of Sophocles possibly in the second century B.C.; Hieronymus of Rhodes, known as an expert on Sophocles' religious beliefs, who in the third century B.C. wrote a volume on famous tragedians; and Carystius of Pergamum, a late second-century B.C. expert on the dramatic prizes Sophocles won. Another, much shorter, version of the playwright's life is found in the *Suidas,* or *Suda Lexicon,* a tenth-century Greek encyclopedia (for a long time scholars incorrectly believed that Suidas was the name of the work's author). The *Suidas* offers a few facts not found in the *Life* and also differs from the latter on certain details, such as the number of prizes the dramatist won.

A WELL-ROUNDED EDUCATION

The consensus of the ancient sources is that Sophocles was born in 497 or 496 B.C. in Colonus, then a village situated about a mile north of Athens's famous central hill, the Acropolis (the site of Colonus now lies inside the city limits). At that time, Attica, the peninsula of eastern Greece dominated and controlled by Athens, was divided into many such villages, called demes. The future playwright's father, Sophillus, perhaps a weapons maker, was evidently wealthy and one of the deme's leading citizens.

Coming from a rich family, it is certain that Sophocles was well-educated. Young, upper-class Greek boys received excellent, well-rounded educations, partly because they were expected eventually to assume leading roles in local government; and this was especially true in Athens, which less than a generation before the dramatist's birth had established the world's first political democracy. The tasks of debating and voting on laws in the liberal and open community Assembly, leading the army, conducting foreign policy, and overseeing the arts, which were largely community and state supported, demanded that such leaders be highly informed and versatile individuals. It is likely that the young Sophocles became well versed in music and literature, which he would later so skillfully exploit, in large degree because the education that he and many other young boys enjoyed stressed both subjects. As noted scholar C.A. Robinson comments:

> He began his training on small scale in the deme ... where local affairs were freely discussed in the town meeting, and where local offices gave some practice in communal manage-

ment. Further experience he gained in one or more of the
many administrative offices of the state and [Athenian] empire, and in the Assembly and law courts. But this practical instruction was narrow. [He] received a broader education from
the [religious] choral songs and festivals and particularly from
the drama presented in the theater. During the year more than
sixty days were [devoted] to festivals, including dramatic exhibitions and the holidays of the demes. Every year, moreover,
from one to two thousand boys appeared before the public in
choruses for the dramatic and other exhibitions that required
them. These choral services . . . were generally rotated among
the qualified citizens, thus giving all, or nearly all, a training
in music and a close contact with literature.

Granted these general activities, the *Life* is more specific
about Sophocles' own education, claiming that he studied
music under Lampros, the most distinguished musician of
his time, and that the boy won prizes for both music and
wrestling. This suggests that Sophocles early embraced and
admirably exemplified the mind-body ethic, a characteristi-
cally Greek philosophy of life that advocated a harmonious
combination of physical and intellectual pursuits. There is
also some evidence that he studied drama under Aeschylus,
the world's first great playwright and by far the most dominant figure in Greek theater in the first decades of the fifth
century B.C. In any case, the young man probably acted in
the choruses of some of Aeschylus's early plays and thereby
"learned the ropes" of the then relatively new and uniquely
Athenian institution of the theater.

INNOVATIVE DEVICES AND UNIVERSAL CONCEPTS

As an innovative artist, Sophocles was fortunate to have
grown up when theater was still in its young and formative
stages. Formal drama had evolved in the mid- to late-sixth
century B.C. from the dithyramb, a traditional and stately religious procession that was part of the celebrations honoring
Dionysus, god of fertility, the change of the seasons, wine,
and religious ecstasy. Ceremonies in which costumed worshipers acted out myths and stories connected with Dionysus
and other gods drew huge audiences from all walks of life.

Eventually, an enterprising dithyrambic performer named
Thespis got the bright idea of having one worshiper stand
separate from and interact with the rest of the group. From
this creation of the first actor and dramatic chorus, the theater was born. Thespis and his colleagues continued to experiment, introducing theatrical conventions such as formal

plays with a prologue and dialogue, musical and dance numbers (at first in imitation of the dithyramb), and masks to represent specific kinds of characters, such as old men, young women, gods, and mythical creatures. They also instituted the grand City Dionysia dramatic festival, held each year at the end of March. Here, for five or six days, playwrights presented their works, the best (or at least the most popular) of which won prizes. Thespis himself is said to have won the grand prize in 534 B.C.

Thus, when Sophocles was born some of the original "founding" playwrights and actors were still living. As he grew up and took part in the great Dionysia, he witnessed continuing innovative theatrical experimentation. In particular, Aeschylus introduced the device of a second actor. Up to that time, playwrights had limited themselves to telling fairly simple stories with two or three characters, which a lone actor tried to portray by repeatedly changing masks. Adding a second actor greatly expanded the scope of the stories writers could present because it allowed them to depict twice as many characters. The potential of this innovation was not lost on Sophocles, who as a young man was undoubtedly already entertaining the concept of a third actor. Aeschylus also introduced the trilogy, or series of three plays related in plot and theme (the world's first sequels). By allowing a story to unfold in three successive plays, he was able to develop concepts such as greed, justice, or fate in more detail.

Such universal concepts, Sophocles learned early on, were integral themes in the myths that playwrights used as a basis for their plots and characters. These traditional stories depicting the interactions of human heroes and villains with various gods and supernatural forces appealed to and fascinated Greek audiences for more than just religious reasons. Charles Segal, a classical scholar and expert on ancient Greek drama, explains:

> At a time when there was no other form of historical record, [the myths] were the repository [storage house] of the past and retained the memory of great events and noteworthy deeds. These tales also embodied the values and concerns central to the society. The Homeric epics [the *Iliad* and *Odyssey*, supposedly composed by the legendary poet Homer about the Trojan War and its aftermath] in particular provided models for heroic behavior and the ideal warrior and ruler, especially in an aristocratic society. . . . The tragedies,

presented to the entire citizen body at the great civic festivals, were not just a major event in Athenian cultural life but were also a kind of mirror in which the city could view itself from the perspective of the whole heroic tradition and the values, ideals, and modes of behavior crystallized in the myths.

When Sophocles himself eventually began transforming popular myths into plays, he used these familiar stories to focus his audience's attention on important political and social themes, such as questions about a person's responsibility to family and community or the conflict between the private and the public good. *Oedipus the King*, for example, opens with a community in crisis and its leader, the title character, facing the responsibility of taking decisive action to end the emergency. What Oedipus does not know, but Sophocles' audience knows full well, is that the action he takes will bring about his personal downfall.

Because the plays' sources were so well known, Greek audiences already knew their outcomes before they entered the theater. Yet that did not diminish their enjoyment of the productions. Modern audiences usually prefer some measure of novelty and surprise in such entertainment; by contrast, the spectators at Sophocles' plays saw the familiar tales as the best possible vehicles for exploring what interested them most—the most profound of human issues, including justice and injustice, good and evil, and the meaning of suffering.

MUCH MORE THAN A PLAYWRIGHT

Eventually, acting in the choruses of Aeschylus and other playwrights, as well as hearing the applause and adulation of the audiences, inspired Sophocles to begin turning out his own plays. It is uncertain when he wrote and produced his first theatrical work; what *is* certain is that he won his first victory in the City Dionysia in 468 B.C., when he was about twenty-eight, for a play titled *Triptolemus*. The twenty-one surviving short fragments of this play are unfortunately insufficient to piece together the plot. But it is safe to assume from the title that it dealt in some way with the myth of Triptolemus. In the story, Triptolemus, a prince of ancient Attica, is chosen by the goddess Demeter to teach his fellow humans how to cultivate grain. According to the famous first-century A.D. Greek writer Plutarch in his *Life of Cimon*, the play's premiere was controversial because of an intense rivalry between Sophocles' supporters and those of the then reigning master, Aeschylus. The archon, or administrator, of the dramatic contests broke with tradition and called upon Cimon, a popular politician and general, to pick a winner.

> When Sophocles, who was still a young man, presented his first trilogy, Apsephion the archon noticed that the spirit of rivalry and partisanship was running high among the audience and decided not to appoint the judges of the contest by lot [random drawing], as was usually done. Instead, when Cimon and his fellow-generals entered the theater and made the usual libation [sacrificial offering of wine or other liquids] to the god Dionysus, he did not allow them to leave, but obliged them to take the oath and sit as judges. . . . In consequence, the fact that the judges were so distinguished raised the whole contest to a far more ambitious level. Sophocles won the prize, and it is said that Aeschylus was so distressed and indignant that he . . . [retired] in anger to Sicily.

Plutarch's reference to Sophocles' "first trilogy" is probably incorrect, for scholars think it more likely that the play in question was part of a tetralogy. An innovation credited to Sophocles himself, this was a group of four plays written, and usually produced, by the same dramatist. Three were tragedies having unrelated subjects and the fourth was a "satyr play," a shorter, comic, and often obscene takeoff on a well-known myth or other popular tale; the purpose of the latter was to provide the audience with some measure of relief from the emotionally draining tragedies. This combination of plays thereafter became the most common. Typically, the five-to-six-day Dionysia festival would feature a tetralogy by each of three playwrights—twelve plays in all.

The tetralogy was only one of many innovations introduced by Sophocles, who vigorously carried on the custom of theatrical experimentation handed down from Thespis and Aeschylus. Sophocles also introduced a third actor, a device that Aeschylus and other writers then began using in many of their own plays. With three actors alternating characters, a dramatist could show more characters and therefore tell a more complex story (evidence suggests that Sophocles carried this idea a step further near the end of his career by utilizing a fourth actor).

Indeed, Sophocles typically stressed character development, often focusing on his leading characters' mix of personal traits and motivations—both good and bad, strong and weak—that influenced their struggles to deal with profound ethical dilemmas. In keeping with this approach, he frequently treated the fifteen-member chorus as a character in its own right. The renowned fourth-century B.C. Greek philosopher-scholar Aristotle praised Sophocles in his *Poetics* for having the chorus participate directly in the action of the story rather than stay primarily in the background.

Other innovations attributed to Sophocles involved costumes, scenery, and props. For example, Aristotle claimed that Sophocles introduced the technique of scene painting. Before Sophocles' time, theater stages, which consisted of an eighty-eight-foot-wide circular orchestra (or "dancing area"), backed by a wooden *skene*, or scene building (with one or more doors for exits and entrances), were mostly bare. Therefore, audiences were expected to imagine the setting or settings of the play's story. Painting or decorating the immovable *skene* to represent the exterior of a palace, a temple, or some other locale added color and a touch of realism to the presentation. However, no evidence has yet been found that Sophocles or any of his colleagues used movable painted scenery like that employed in modern theaters. In addition, the *Life* credits Sophocles with introducing various props for the actors. These and other similar contributions show us that Sophocles was much more than a mere playwright; rather, he was often the play's producer, director, a chorus member or extra, and in addition, writes scholar and translator Lane Cooper,

> his own stage manager. He ... trained his chorus and actors, and, with the help of a costumer, attended to their garb, masks, padding, and footwear. In the great theater, his persons [had to be] of heroic mold and stature ... [so they were] carefully drilled in declamation [so they could] be heard by an immense, and sometimes noisy, audience. ... The actors spoke most of their lines, yet delivered some others in an intoned chant, and sang the more lyrical passages in solos, or in duet or trios; or again, they joined with the chorus in a song. ... Their statuesque poses and measured [dances] had the greatest share in producing the whole amazing spectacle of Attic drama. ... The dramatist, then, had to be poet, musician, and expert in pantomimic dancing as well. ... Sophocles was all of these things and more.

POSITIONS OF POWER AND RESPONSIBILITY

Sophocles continued to distinguish himself as a versatile writer-producer-director in the Athenian dramatic festivals for six decades. The titles, dates, and order of appearance of the plays he produced in the twenty years following the premiere of *Triptolemus* are largely unknown; the first of his seven surviving tragedies, *Ajax*, was first presented in about 447 B.C. In this play, Sophocles explored the changes in personal and ethical codes that had occurred in the transition from the primitive society of the legendary Trojan War era to his own society. The title character, along with Achilles, Odysseus, and the other Greek generals who laid siege to Troy, were larger-than-life, heroic yet aristocratic, arrogant, and self-serving figures who totally dominated their respective communities. They would have been very out of place in the more democratic city-states of Sophocles' time, in which each citizen, no matter how poor his origins, was viewed as worthy.

The legendary events leading up to the beginning of the play took place near the end of the long siege of Troy and shortly after the death of Achilles, the mightiest of the Greek leaders. The other generals vied for his weapons and armor and Ajax, recognized as the second mightiest of their number, laid the strongest claim. But the shrewd Odysseus was awarded the prizes instead, after which the enraged Ajax vowed to get revenge on all concerned. In the opening scene, the goddess Athena tells Odysseus how she thwarted Ajax from this bloodletting by afflicting him with temporary madness; in this state, he mistook a herd of cows for his enemies and slaughtered the beasts. Now, the mighty hero, having realized his mistake, sits mortified and contemplating suicide in his tent. In the course of the play, he recognizes that his world is changing, that soon there will no longer be room for heroic but vain, ignorant, and ultimately destructive men like himself. And so, bemoaning the ravages of time and fate, he eventually falls on his sword.

In the years following the premiere of *Ajax*, Sophocles periodically found himself serving in positions of lofty power and responsibility not unlike those held by the characters in the play. In 443 B.C., Pericles, Athens's most popular and powerful politician, appointed him *Hellenotamias*, the chief treasurer in charge of collecting money from the member states of the far-flung Athenian empire. Athens ruled this federation with a heavy hand and many of these cities paid the tribute only because of the very real threat of punitive measures by the Athenian army and navy; therefore, Sophocles' office was one of considerable power and importance.

The dramatist achieved an even more powerful post three

years later when he was elected one of Athens's ten *strategoi,* the military generals who commanded the armies and carried out state foreign policy. With Pericles the dominant general, Sophocles and the others led a fleet of more than two hundred warships in a brutally successful nine-month siege of the island city-state of Samos, which had made the mistake of challenging Athens's authority. Some evidence suggests that the playwright was elected to another one-year term as general in 415, when he was eighty-one. According to Plutarch, for instance, when Athens's fleet was laying siege to the Greek Sicilian city of Syracuse and the Athenian generals were discussing an important matter, the commander, Nicias, "called upon Sophocles, as the senior officer on board, to give his opinion first, to which Sophocles replied: 'I may be the oldest man here, but you are the senior general.'" There is some lingering doubt about this story, however, partly because the *Life* states that Sophocles' second generalship occurred when he was sixty-nine, which would date his service to 427, long before the Syracusan expedition. Still more evidence indicates that he may have served in 413 as *proboulus,* or high commissioner, to help with the emergency following the sudden collapse of that ill-fated expedition.

THE UNRELENTING WORKINGS OF FATE

Whatever the number and dates of Sophocles' stints in public office, there can be little doubt that they came as the result of the great popularity he earned as a playwright. For example, his election to *strategos* in 440 B.C. was almost certainly due to the notoriety surrounding the great success of *Antigone* the year before. This play was the author's first dealing with the Oedipus cycle of myths, although the events depicted here occur long after those of *Oedipus the King,* written later. After Oedipus's downfall and abdication of the throne of Thebes, his son, Polynices, died battling his own brother. Their uncle, Creon, having succeeded to the throne, forbade anyone from burying Polynices' body, an act that the ancient Greeks, who were extremely concerned with proper burial rites, considered horrendously cruel. As the play opens, the dead man's sister, Antigone, in defiance of the king, endeavors to bury the body. But Creon catches her in the act and condemns her to be buried alive in a sealed cave. Haemon, Creon's son and Antigone's betrothed, having failed to change his father's mind, rushes to the cave to die with Antigone. The king finally relents, but it is too late; reaching the cave he finds that Antigone has hung herself, and before his eyes Haemon also commits suicide.

Here, Sophocles touched a nerve that fascinated and moved his audiences. The core of the play was the dramatic confrontation between the laws enacted by state and society and those larger and more eternal natural laws that are the birthright of all human beings. Through the spectacle of Antigone's courage and sacrifice, the playwright seemed to be saying that even though Creon was king, he had no right to deny another person certain fundamental elements of human dignity. Indeed, *Antigone* stands as one of Western literature's greatest hymns to human worth and dignity. "Wonders there are many," sings the play's chorus, "but none more wonderful than human beings."

The next time Sophocles addressed the Oedipus cycle was in his masterpiece, *Oedipus the King*, which premiered about 429. The story was well known to his audiences, of course. After hearing from an oracle that he would kill his father and marry his mother, Oedipus fled from Corinth to Thebes, over which he soon became ruler. Years later, after he had married Jocasta, the former king's wife, and had children by her, a terrible plague struck Thebes. As the play opens, Oedipus seeks a way to lift the plague. He comes to believe that the pestilence was sent by the gods as a punishment for the murder of Jocasta's first husband, an event that occurred shortly before Oedipus himself first arrived in Thebes. Oedipus vows to find and punish this murderer. But as the terrible events unfold, he discovers to his horror that he himself is the culprit; an old man he slew at a crossroads on the way to Thebes was, it turns out, King Laius, Jocasta's husband. Even worse, Jocasta and Laius are his real parents, which means that the old prophecy he had tried to escape has come true. On learning the hideous truth, Jocasta hangs herself and Oedipus gashes out his own eyes.

Years later, Aristotle singled out the play as a model of great tragic drama. Critics through the ages have almost unanimously agreed, calling attention to the skillful way that Sophocles showed the inevitable and unrelenting workings of fate and the ways a character's own arrogance and ignorance can bring about his or her ultimate downfall. In light of the praise heaped on the work after the author's death, it is interesting to note that it did not win the first prize when it was presented at the Dionysia festival. *Oedipus the King* came in a disappointing second to a play by Philocles, the nephew of Aeschylus. No doubt the playwrights themselves were subject to the workings of fate, which ultimately immortalized the loser and condemned the winner to obscurity.

THE MIRE OF HUMAN PASSIONS

A year or two after presenting *Oedipus the King*, Sophocles wrote *The Women of Trachis*. This play depicts a dramatic episode in the life of the legendary hero Heracles (sometimes referred to as Hercules). His wife, Deianira, is consumed by jealousy after hearing that he has taken a mistress, and in the process of trying to win back his love she unwittingly poisons him. He eventually dies and their son, Hyllus, angrily blames the gods. Indeed, thinking Heracles too self-centered, overconfident, and brazenly insolent toward them, several of the gods have conspired against him and Deianira to ensure his downfall. Like Oedipus, Heracles is, to a large degree, a victim of forces greater than himself and beyond his control.

Sophocles touched on another part of the Heracles mythos, or group of myths, in *Philoctetes*, a play that also dealt with the Trojan War, a subject explored in *Ajax*. In *Philoctetes*, produced in 409 B.C., when the playwright was eighty-seven, the title character is a warrior who, after suffering a snakebite, is left behind on the island of Lemnos by the Greek army on its way to Troy. Having come into possession of Heracles' mighty bow and arrows, Philoctetes manages to keep from starving in the nine years he spends on the island. In the play's opening, Odysseus, accompanied by Achilles' son, Neoptolemus, arrives on Lemnos looking for the lost warrior. A soothsayer had foretold that the Greeks could not win the war against Troy without Philoctetes and Heracles' bow. After a bout of rivalry and intrigue between Philoctetes and Neoptolemus, Heracles, now a god, intervenes and orders the men to return to Troy and conclude the siege.

Sometime between his production of these two plays dealing with Heracles, perhaps in about 415, Sophocles wrote *Electra*. Like *The Women of Trachis*, *Electra* deals with intrigues and deaths among family members; but in this case the dramatic and bloody events are driven more by the vengeance of humans than of the gods. Orestes, prince of the royal house of Mycenae, a family that has long endured a terrible curse of hatred and bloodshed, arrives home wearing a disguise. His plan is to kill his mother, Clytemnestra, and her lover, for the murder of Orestes' father, Agamemnon. Orestes' sister Electra, who already hates her mother and the usurper of her father's throne, is further grieved when the young man, pretending to be a stranger, presents an urn of ashes and claims they are his own remains. Having gained the queen's confidence, Orestes kills his mother and her lover, and then reveals himself to Electra, after which the chorus expresses the hope that the family curse will be broken.

Sophocles' audiences must have identified strongly with many of the characters in *Electra*. The vengeful Orestes, adulterous Clytemnestra, and grieving Electra displayed many strengths and weaknesses, and expressed many emotions—love, hate, courage, helplessness—with which average Athenians were familiar in their own lives. Aeschylus, too, had dealt with the Orestes story in his famous trilogy, the *Oresteia*; but in his version the killing of Clytemnestra and other dramatic events are seen as the result of inescapable destiny, overseen by the gods on high. Sophocles brought the action back down to earth and rooted the violence in the mire of human passions.

A GENTLEMAN ALWAYS

The passions and emotions that drove the playwright himself remain largely unknown. Although the *Life*, the *Suidas*, Plutarch's biographies, and other sources provide us with some information about his public life in the theater and government service, little is known about his private life and personal character. His colleague, the famous comic playwright Aristophanes, provided a clue in his play *Frogs*, produced shortly after Sophocles' death. The gods Dionysus and Heracles, portrayed comically in the play, discuss Dionysus's desire to bring the playwright Euripides back from the dead. "Why resurrect Euripides instead of Sophocles?" Heracles asks. Dionysus answers, "Euripides, the clever rogue, would aid my kidnap scheme; while Sophocles, gentleman always, is a gentleman still." Since Aristophanes knew Sophocles personally, we can be fairly certain of the accuracy of this description.

Indeed, there are other brief references in ancient sources suggesting that Sophocles was a gentle, caring, and pious individual. Apparently he was a priest, or at least a devout worshiper, of several healing deities, most notably Asclepius. According to one ancient writer, Sophocles composed a hymn of praise to Asclepius, a work that became very popular in Athens. Also, the playwright supposedly erected a shrine to Heracles, the stalwart, if overbearing, mortal-turned-god who figured so importantly in several of his plays.

As to Sophocles' family relationships, he was married at least once. His wife, Nicostrate, bore him a son, Iophon, who himself became a tragic poet. The *Suidas* mentions several other sons about which nothing is known. Sophocles also had a grandson of the same name who wrote some forty plays and won several dramatic competitions; and in the third century B.C. another of his descendants bearing the name of Sophocles wrote at least fifteen tragedies.

Sophocles' friends no doubt included most if not all of the prominent artists and writers, as well as the political leaders, of his age. After all, Athens was not a large city and the dramatist was a leading figure in both artistic and political circles. The *Life* suggests that he was on good terms with his younger colleague, Euripides, whom he outlived, and a tragic poet named Ion of Chios seems to have been another close acquaintance. In addition, there is considerable evidence that he had a close friendship with the historian Herodotus, whom later scholars came to call the "father of history." Plutarch recorded a few lines from a song written by Sophocles in honor of Herodotus, and several of Sophocles' plays contain historical and geographical information apparently borrowed directly from the historian's famous book *The Histories*, before it was finished.

A LONG AND FULFILLING LIFE

As it turned out, Sophocles outlived Herodotus, too, along with Pericles, Nicias, and the other generals with whom he had once proudly served; in fact, the playwright may have outlived almost all of his relatives and friends, for he lived to be at least ninety-one. Yet even in his last years, his creative talent and output were not in the least diminished, for his last play, *Oedipus at Colonus*, composed in 406 B.C., was one of his greatest. About this beautiful and mysterious play, respected classical historian Michael Grant writes:

The story is a sequel of *Oedipus the King*, at the end of which he had blinded himself and departed from Thebes. Now a ragged beggar, after years of wandering from place to place, he arrives at Colonus, near Athens, led by his daughter Antigone. The elders of Colonus, the chorus of the play, go to see him but are horror-struck when they learn who he is, and order him to leave.... [However] King Theseus promises to help him, and frustrates Creon, who has arrived from Thebes to seize both the blind former monarch and Antigone (her sister Ismene has already been captured).... Thunderclaps tell Oedipus that his hour has come, and attended by Theseus and his daughters he leads the way to a place where he will depart from the land of the living. Halfway he bids Antigone and Ismene farewell, and what happened next no one but Theseus knew; but, according to a messenger's report, Oedipus was taken by the gods.

In a way, the ending of *Oedipus at Colonus* was ironic and prophetic, for Sophocles himself was "taken by the gods" very shortly after completing the play. The cause of death, despite much speculation by later scholars, remains unknown; but considering his advanced age, natural causes seem most likely. The great dramatist left behind an enormous legacy, of which the modern world has inherited but a small fraction, although the contents of that fraction are indeed an astonishing artistic achievement. All that has survived of his lost plays are the titles, mentioned in the books of ancient historians, or brief fragments, usually comprising no more than a few lines and often no more than a few words. The remains of his play *Alexander*, for example, consist of a mere three lines and six individual words; of *The Captives*, thirteen partial lines and thirteen single words; of *The Daedalus*, two single lines, two two-word combinations, and two single words; of *The Tantalus*, just a single line; of *Clytemnestra*, *Euryalus*, and *The Theseus*, nothing at all; and the list goes on and on. The lone exception is one of Sophocles' satyr plays, *Ichneutae*, or *The Trackers*. After some four hundred lines of this work were discovered in an Egyptian papyrus in the early 1900s, scholars were able to piece together the plot.

That many of these lost plays were at least as great as Sophocles' seven surviving works cannot be doubted. The proof is his record of victories in the dramatic contests, one unmatched by any other playwright in the long history of the Greek festivals. Ancient sources all agree that he won the great Dionysia competition at least eighteen times, and no less than six other victories are recorded for other contests. Moreover, states the *Life,* although the judges often awarded him second place, he never once came in third.

These numerous victories, along with decades of applause, praise, and expressions of trust and appreciation by his countrymen, must have pleased Sophocles greatly and capped a long, prosperous, creative, and fulfilling life. The comic playwright Phrynichus summed it up well in these words of tribute from his play *Muses,* produced just a few months after the master tragedian's death: "Happy Sophocles, who died after a long life, fortunate, clever, who composed many beautiful tragedies and died happily without having experienced any evil." Fortunate, indeed, are the audiences of succeeding generations, as well, who were, are, and always will be indebted to Sophocles for a life exceedingly well spent.

CHAPTER 1

Sophocles the Dramatist

READINGS ON
SOPHOCLES

Sophocles' Use of Mythology

C.M. Bowra

Sophocles, like his fellow dramatists Aeschylus and Euripides, regularly drew upon Greek mythology for plots and characters for his plays. This practice stemmed not from a lack of inventiveness, but rather from a realization that his audiences were steeped in these ancient tales of the gods and the mortal heroes who interacted with them. Indeed, as C.M. Bowra, one of the twentieth century's most respected classical scholars, explains here, the myths were a living part of the consciousness of the average person, who felt "perfectly at home with them." These stories were instructive, says Bowra, in that they often suggested or showed correct ways of conduct or courses of action. People saw lessons in the mistakes made by the human characters in the myths and at the same time thought about and clarified their own relationships with the gods. Also, to Greek theater audiences many of the characters portrayed in the plays were not simply symbolic or remote figures; instead, they were omnipresent, that is, lurking always somewhere nearby, in some supernatural state, observing or even guarding the living. In this way, Oedipus was not only a fascinating character in Sophocles' plays, but also an unseen presence who continued to watch over Athens. Just as he was redeemed in the sight of the gods, so too, Athenians believed, their city might be redeemed. Thus, to witness these old stories replayed on Athenian stages was a compelling, powerful, and emotional experience.

The abiding concern of the Greeks with humanity was largely the result of the heroic tradition of poetry, and it was all the more secure because this tradition was deeply interested in the dealings of men with gods and implicitly with the worth of human actions and the notion that a man should exert

From C.M. Bowra, *The Greek Experience* (London: Weidenfeld & Nicolson, 1957). Reprinted with permission of the publisher.

himself to the utmost with his natural powers. If myths gave instruction, they did so in a generous spirit, with no attempt to preach. They helped to form character by clarifying issues of conduct in their dramatic presentation of them and in showing the place of man in the universe by telling of his relations with the gods. . . .

THE OLD STORIES TOLD AGAIN

This straightforward handling of myths fixed them in the Greek consciousness, made it feel perfectly at home with them, and rely on them to illustrate or justify different courses of behaviour, and prepared the way for developments in which they could be used with a more special intention. As the heroic ideal was transformed to suit the demands of the city-state, the Greeks turned their myths to more complex purposes. With the vast achievement of the epic [poem, for example Homer's *Iliad* and *Odyssey*] behind them, and in the sure confidence that its stories were more or less familiar to everyone, they could read more into them, treat them more allusively, and use them to dramatize those issues of life and death which awoke their eager and profound consideration. The three Attic [referring to Attica, the peninsula on which Athens is located] tragedians, Aeschylus, Sophocles, and Euripides, all used familiar myths for their tragedies, and nearly always drew on heroic stories. This too was an exalted art, to which nothing common or mean could be admitted. Greek tragedy was not always tragic in the modern sense; it did not necessarily end in disaster. In this it reflected the epic, which dealt indeed with disasters but realized its essence in a sense of the urgency and importance of human action. Attic tragedy is no less serious, and is in this respect the rightful heir of epic. But instead of aiming exclusively at exalted enjoyment, it sought to make its effects more impressive by relating them to fundamental issues in the relations of gods with men. Perhaps this was inevitable in an art which was performed at the festival of a god, but it is no less likely to have been due to the Athenian spirit, which believed that men are inextricably connected with the gods, and wished to explore this connexion with a bold and searching curiosity. Myth provided the framework of drama, which illustrated in a highly concrete and cogent way some important crisis or problem, and that is why Greek tragedy can be called symbolical. The old stories are indeed told again for their own sake, and there is no lack of dramatic tension and human interest, but they also exemplify some far-reaching problem, which is admirably presented in this individual shape. The heroes of the past keep their individuality, but also become types of human destiny and examples of men's dealings with the gods. Each man may see in them something which concerns himself, and though their presentation is always exciting and gives its own kind of pleasure, behind and beyond this lies some universal issue which is made more significant by the special form in which it is embodied. . . .

The Attic tragedians were deeply concerned with current problems. They saw them, indeed, with a lofty detachment, but they none the less thought that what mattered for their own generation was the right material for tragedy. They transposed the disturbing problems and the passionate disputes of the Athenian democracy to the world of ancient myth and gave to them a distance and a dignity which made their issues clearer and set them above the confusions of ephemeral controversy. Torn from their contemporary context, these questions are revealed in their ultimate urgency and given a new life through the myths which enfold them. . . .

VIOLENT ACTION AND INCOMPARABLE SONG

Since tragedy was a vehicle for displaying the nature of religious experience, it often dealt with questions and misgivings which assail men about the gods. In the *Prometheus Bound*, which is the first of three plays about the Titan Prometheus, who helped men by stealing fire from heaven and on the orders of Zeus was bound for it to a mountain, . . . Aeschylus faces the whole metaphysics of power which makes the gods what they are, and asks what it means in human terms. Zeus, who punishes Prometheus, is presented as an upstart tyrant; Prometheus, the friend of men, is a patient, outspoken, unyielding martyr. Our sympathies are almost wholly with him, since his compassion for the pathetic helplessness and ignorance of men is in sharp contrast with the heartless unconcern of Zeus. Aeschylus surely means us to feel this, but it is only one side of the picture; the other side was developed in the two lost plays, in which Zeus in the end released Prometheus and showed that the fulfilment of power is in reason and justice. In these plays Aeschylus transposed to a cosmic stage something which was disturbingly apparent in the new and vigorous democracy of Athens. After the Persian Wars, Athens tasted power and thirsted for more, and in the process lost some of its first generosity. Just as it soon began to use force against those allies who refused to submit to its will, so it turned on its own saviours and benefactors, like Themistocles and Aristides [popular leaders who fell from favor and were banished], because it was suspicious of their independence and candour. Aeschylus knew this, but saw far beyond it, and realized that it raised universal issues, which he made the subject of his drama.

With this play of the expanding Athenian Empire we may compare another which comes from its close. Sophocles wrote his *Oedipus at Colonus* soon before his death in 406 B.C., when the end of Athens was near and the long struggle

---

THE ANCIENT MYTH OF OEDIPUS

In these comments excerpted from his controversial book, Oedipus and Akhnaton: Myth and History, *the noted scholar Immanuel Velikovsky speaks about the great age of the Oedipus myth.*

The earliest reference to the Oedipus legend is found in Homer's *Odyssey.* The epic was most probably put into writing early in the seventh century before the present era; it describes the travels and wanderings of Odysseus after the fall of Troy, in the siege of which he had participated. The wanderer also visited Hades, the abode of the departed. There he saw the unfortunate mother-wife of Oedipus; Homer called her Epicaste:

"And I saw the mother of Oedipodes, fair Epicaste, who wrought a monstrous deed in ignorance of mind in that she wedded her own son, and he, when he had slain his own father, wedded her, and straightway the gods made these things known among men. . . . She made fast a noose on high from a lofty beam, overpowered by her sorrow."

It is generally accepted that the Oedipus cycle of legends is of greater antiquity than the so-called Homeric cycle of the siege of Troy by the Greeks or Achaeans under Agamemnon, and older, too, than the time of the Tyrants, Thyestes and his brother Atreus, father of Agamemnon. The inclusion of a short reference to the Oedipus tragedy in the *Odyssey* permits us to deduce only that the legend is older than the seventh century, the time when the Homeric epics were put into writing.

with Sparta [a powerful rival city-state] could only end in defeat. He chose his subject from local myth, from rites paid near Athens at Colonus to Oedipus as a demi-god who lived under the earth and was believed to have recently helped the Athenians in war. Sophocles' play tells of the end of Oedipus. The old man, blind and worn by much suffering, comes to a grove at Colonus and knows that his wanderings are over and his end is near. He prepares for his passing, and in his last ordeals he displays with increasing force the qualities of the demi-god which he is destined soon to become, until at last a voice calls him from the sky and, despite his blindness, he moves away unaided and disappears from the world of men. The play is rich in violent action and incomparable song, but it is shaped by the notion of an unseen presence which watches over Athens. Sophocles is concerned to show what a demi-god really is, and gives to Oedipus a terrifying majesty and force of passion. He conforms to the belief that such beings love their friends and hate their enemies; and that is why Oedipus both shows a loving solicitude for his daughters, who have been faithful to him in his sufferings, and an unforgiving savagery for those who have wronged him, like his treacherous son Polynices. Above all, in his friendship with Theseus, the king of Athens, he forecasts how after death he will protect Athens from the earth where he abides. Sophocles understood Greek religious experience, and in this play faced one of its more mysterious articles of belief. Because his myth is so clearly conceived, he is able to show what a demi-god means to those who honour him.

THE GODS HUMBLE THE GREAT

In these two cases the poets almost point out a moral, or at least propound both a problem and their solution for it. But this was not necessary, and perhaps not even usual. One of the chief functions of tragedy was to present in concrete form issues that concerned men in their relations with the gods and with one another. In almost every extant play there is behind the individual action a universal situation or problem or question, which is presented in such a way that we see what it really means for human beings. The selection which the poet makes from mythology provides him not only with a dramatic subject but with a means to clarify something that absorbs or troubles his mind. The strength of his play arises largely from the degree in which he has thought and felt about this and what it means in terms of human action. Even if he has a solution for it, this is usually much less important imaginatively and poetically than the presentation of the situation which provokes it. For instance, in *King Oedipus* Sophocles faces the problem of a gifted and noble man, who through no fault of his own is hideously humbled and suffers a ghastly fate. He hints, indeed, that there is a solution for this, that the gods humble the great because they wish to warn men against the dangers of power and position, but this is kept till the end and has very little part in the play. What counts in the dramatic action is the appalling emotional impact which it has on us and which forces us to sympathize, in the full sense of the word, with Oedipus in his tragic situation and to think for ourselves about it. The drama moves in a world in which men think that they know something about themselves and their destinies, but they are the victims of illusion. They know nothing, and in the end the gods force the truth upon them. This is not a lesson, but a state of mind . . . impressed on us by the power of poetry and by the myth which Sophocles uses. In its simplest form the fall of Oedipus is that of a man who falls from prosperity to adversity, and the myth provides this for the poet to make use of. What he does is not only to dramatize it in such a way that every word and action makes an impression on us, but to show the frame of mind in which such a fall is possible, the errors which beset a powerful and successful man like Oedipus, and the even greater errors into which they lead him. Nor is this technique merely an adroit exploitation of a given myth; it is in itself a reflection of the mythical way of thinking. The issues which Sophocles dramatizes are best presented not as intellectual abstractions, but as living states of mind which we all know in ourselves and which become more urgent and more vivid when we see them on the stage. By relying upon myths for their plots, the Greek dramatists are able not merely to provide a stirring drama but to communicate to us something whose whole character and significance can be revealed only by this imaginative identification of the universal problem with the individual case.

Sophocles' Mastery of Character Development

Werner Jaeger

In this excerpt from his insightful study of ancient Greek culture and thought, *Paideia: The Ideals of Greek Culture*, former Harvard University professor Werner Jaeger discusses what many scholars see as Sophocles' greatest single theatrical talent: character development. Jaeger argues that unlike Aeschylus, who dealt with human suffering by showing how entire generations of a family or society are guilty and should be punished, Sophocles usually focused more closely on the suffering of specific individuals. Sophocles demonstrated the terrible personal toll exacted when individual men and women, through ignorance, arrogance, or both, make mistakes that bring the wrath of the gods down on themselves and their families. More often than not, he first introduced these characters as ideal and larger-than-life individuals, rather than as realistic everyday people, so that when they are inevitably knocked from their pedestals they have that much farther to fall.

The ineffaceable [lasting] impression which Sophocles makes on us today and his imperishable position in the literature of the world are both due to his character-drawing. If we ask which of the men and women of Greek tragedy have an independent life in the imagination apart from the stage and from the actual plot in which they appear, we must answer, 'those created by Sophocles, above all others'. He was much more than a technician: for characters which *live* cannot be created by mere excellence in dramatic technique, which has at best a temporary effect. Perhaps nothing is harder for us to understand than the quiet, unpretentious, natural wisdom of Sophocles, which makes us feel that his

Excerpted from Werner Jaeger, *Paideia: The Ideals of Greek Culture*, vol. 1, translated from the 2nd German edition by Gilbert Highet (New York: Oxford University Press, 1945). Reprinted by permission of Blackwell Publishers, Oxford, U.K.

real flesh-and-blood men and women, with violent passions and tender emotions, proudly heroic but truly human, are like ourselves and yet noble with an incomparable dignity and remoteness. There is no sophistical subtlety, no artificial exaggeration about these characters. Later ages [of theatrical writers and producers] vainly tried to achieve monumental sublimity [nobility] by violence, by colossal size and startling effects. Sophocles found sublimity in the effortless calm of true proportion: for it is always simple and even obvious. Its secret lies in the abandonment of everything inessential and accidental, so that nothing is left but the perfect clarity of that inner law which is hidden from the outward eye. The men created by Sophocles have none of the earthy compactness of Aeschylus' characters, who look impassive, even stiff, beside them; nor is their mobility spoilt by lack of balance, as in so many of Euripides' puppets—it is hard to call them characters, since they never grow beyond the two dimensions of the theatre, costume and declamation, and never round out into real physical presences. . . .

A MOMENT UNIQUE IN HISTORY

Many writers have drawn parallels between poetry and sculpture, and compared each of the three tragedians with one stage in the development of plastic art. . . . But when we call Sophocles the sculptor of tragedy, we mean that he possesses one quality unlike any other poet—a fact which makes it impossible to institute any comparison between the development of tragedy and that of sculpture. . . .

The tragedies of Sophocles and the sculptures of Phidias are the two imperishable monuments of the great age of the Athenian spirit. Together, they represent the art of the Periclean era. Looking backward from the work of Sophocles, one seems to see all the previous development of tragedy as merely leading up to this perfection. Even Aeschylus appears to be only a preparation for Sophocles. . . . Therefore Sophocles is classical, inasmuch as he is the climax of the development of tragedy: in him tragedy 'had its nature', as Aristotle would say. But there is another unique sense in which he is classical: and here that description connotes more than perfection within one literary form. His position in the development of the spirit of Greece makes him classical. . . . The work of Sophocles is the climax of the development of Greek poetry, considered as the process by which the formation of human character is increasingly objectified. From this point of view alone can our ... discussion of his tragic characters be fully understood and even gain additional significance. Their excellence is not in their form alone; it is a more deeply human excellence, for in it aesthetic and moral and religious elements interfuse and interact. Such a fusing of motives is not unique in Greek poetry. ... But in Sophocles' tragedies form and norm are unified in a special sense, and they are unified above all in his characters. He himself said tersely but accurately that his characters were ideals, not ordinary men like those of Euripides. As a creator of men, Sophocles has a place in the history of human culture essentially unlike that of any other Greek poet. In his work the fully awakened sense of culture is made manifest for the first time. It is something totally different from the educational effect of Homer or the educational purpose of Aeschylus. It assumes the existence of a society whose highest ideal is *culture*, the formation of perfect human character; and such an assumption was impossible until, after one entire generation had struggled to discover the meaning of destiny, after the sore spiritual agonies of Aeschylus, humanity itself had become the centre of life. The character-drawing of Sophocles is consciously inspired by that ideal of human conduct which was the peculiar creation of Periclean society and civilization. He assimilated that ideal so fully that he humanized tragedy, and converted it into an imperishable pattern of human culture which was entirely in the inimitable [matchless] spirit of the men who created it. ... Culture was for the Greeks the original creation and original experience of a process of deliberate guidance and formation of human character. Understanding that, we shall also understand the power of such an ideal to inspire the imagination of a great poet. It was a moment unique in the history of the world when poetry and culture came together to create an ideal. ...

A SENSE OF PROPORTION

That ideal was inspired by a clear and delicate perception of correct and appropriate behaviour in every situation, which, despite its precise rules for speech and conduct and its perfect sense of proportion and control, was in effect a new spiritual freedom. Entirely without effort or affectation, it was an easy and unconstrained [liberated] way of life, appreciated and admired by all. ... It existed only in Athens. It meant an abandonment of the exaggerated violence of emotion and expression that characterized Aeschylus, for the miraculously natural poise and proportion which we feel and enjoy in the sculptured frieze of the Parthenon as well as in the language of the men and women of Sophocles. An open secret, it can only be described, not defined; but at least it is not a matter of pure form. After all, it would be too extraordinary if the same phenomenon appeared at the same time in poetry and sculpture without being created by some ... feeling common to all the men who were most characteristic of their age. It is the radiance of a life that has found the final peace and final harmony with itself which are expressed in

ANTIGONE'S DESPAIR

This scene from Antigone, *in which the title character and the chorus discuss her despair and suffering, illustrates Jaeger's point that Sophocles strongly emphasized the problems of the individual.*

CHORUS:
> You have passed beyond human daring and come at last
> Into a place of stone where Justice sits.
> I cannot tell
> What shape of your father's guilt appears in this.

ANTIGONE:
> You have touched it at last: that bridal bed
> Unspeakable, horror of son and mother mingling:
> Their crime, infection of all our family!
> O Oedipus, father and brother!
> Your marriage strikes from the grave to murder mine.
> I have been a stranger here in my own land:
> All my life
> The blasphemy of my birth has followed me.

CHORUS:
> Reverence is a virtue, but strength
> Lives in established law: that must prevail.
> You have made your choice,
> Your death is the doing of your conscious hand.

ANTIGONE:
> Then let me go, since all your words are bitter,
> And the very light of the sun is cold to me.
> Lead me to my vigil, where I must have
> Neither love nor lamentation; no song, but silence.

Aristophanes' description of Sophocles: a life which even the passage through death cannot affect, which remains both 'there' and 'here', content. . . . Sophocles' tragedies are the climax of the development of the Greek idea that proportion is one of the highest values in human life. The process leads up to him, and in him it finds its classical poetic expression as the divine power which rules the world and human life.

There is another way to demonstrate the close connexion between culture and the sense of proportion in the mind of fifth-century Greece. In general we are compelled to draw inferences from the works of the Greek artists to the artistic theories which they held; their works are in fact the principal evidence for their beliefs. But in trying to understand the obscure and yet fundamental principles which assisted in the creation of works of art so many in number and so various in possible interpretations, we are justified in seeking contemporary evidence to guide us. In this context, then, we possess two remarks made by Sophocles himself—which indeed owe their ultimate historical authority only to the fact that they harmonize with our intuitive judgment of his art. We have already quoted one of them, in which Sophocles described his own characters as ideal figures in contrast to Euripidean realism. In the other he distinguished his own work from that of Aeschylus by saying that Aeschylus wrote correctly without knowing why. . . . Both remarks taken together presuppose a very special awareness of standards to be followed: Sophocles guided his work by a standard and in it presented men 'as they ought to be'. . . .

THE DRAMA OF EMOTIONS

We can now understand the changes which tragedy underwent when Sophocles took it over from Aeschylus. The most obvious external change is Sophocles' abandonment of the trilogy, which had been Aeschylus' regular dramatic form. It was now replaced by single dramas, centred on one principal actor. It was impossible for Aeschylus to give dramatic treatment to the connected development of one destiny on the epic scale, often covering the sufferings of several generations of the same family, in anything less than a trilogy of tragedies. His chief concern was the unbroken course of the fate of a family, because it alone formed a whole large enough to demonstrate the working-out of divine justice, which even religious faith and moral sentiment can hardly trace in the doom of one individual. In his plays, therefore, single characters are subordinated to the main theme, although they may serve to introduce the spectator to it; and the poet himself is compelled to assume a higher and less human position, making his puppets move and suffer as if he himself were the power which guides the universe. But in Sophocles the ideal of justifying God's ways to man . . . falls into the background. The tragic element in his plays is the inevitability of suffering: the necessity of destiny, seen from the point of view of the individual sufferer. He has not, therefore, abandoned Aeschylus' religious view of the nature of the world, but has merely shifted the emphasis from universal to individual problems. This is particularly clear in an early work like *Antigone*, where his conception of the meaning of the world is still boldly marked. . . .

Sophocles draws from [his] characters a marvelous and delicate variety of tragical music; and he enhances its searching beauty by every device of the dramatist's imagination. Compared with those of Aeschylus, his plays are an immeasurable advance in dramatic effect. Yet he did not achieve this by abandoning the fine old choric songs and dances and telling a story for its own sake with Shakespearean realism. . . . Sophoclean drama is the drama of the emotions through which the soul of the chief actor must pass, following in its own rhythm the harmonious development of the plot. The source of his dramatic effect is the hero's character, to which, as to the highest and final point of interest, it always returns. Dramatic action is for Sophocles the process by which the true nature of a suffering human being is unfolded, by which he fulfils his destiny, and through it fulfils himself.

Sophocles' Moral Themes

Robert D. Murray Jr.

In the following essay, Robert D. Murray Jr., a former classics professor at Princeton University, explains that scholars often differ over Sophocles' intentions as a playwright. Some, collectively referred to as the "formalists," argue that Sophocles was mainly a craftsman who constructed dazzling and powerful pieces of theater, works that excite and move audiences but that do not attempt to convey any serious message, moral, or underlying meaning. On the other side of the debate are the "moralists," those who feel that Sophocles structured his plays not only for outward show, but also to teach a lesson or convey an idea. In this argument of structure versus thought, Murray ultimately comes down on the side of the moralists. Using the structures and meanings of *Oedipus Tyrannus* and *Oedipus at Colonus* as examples, he shows that in Sophocles' plays structure and thought are not independent of each other; rather, they are interwoven to produce a magnificent unified whole.

Because we are men of the twentieth century and not of the fifth century B.C., there are obviously many obstacles between us and a proper confrontation of Greek tragedy. Not the least of these roadblocks is the fact that as men of the twentieth century we have been exposed often to a critical doctrine that does not meet the facts of the case. This doctrine, paralleled and perhaps even stimulated by movements in music, the fine arts, and philosophy, informs us that we are stumbling into an intellectual bog if we try to look for moral or meaning in a literary work. The projection of a moral view is not centrally a function of the work of art;

Robert D. Murray Jr., "Thought and Structure in Sophoclean Tragedy," in Thomas Woodward, ed., *Sophocles: A Collection of Critical Essays.* Englewood Cliffs, NJ: Prentice-Hall, 1966, pp. 23–28.

after all, if one wishes to convey meaning and morality verbally, this end can be accomplished most precisely and unambiguously through the precision of prose discourse. Poetry, perhaps since Dante [the thirteenth-century Italian author of the *Divine Comedy*], has seldom been regarded as the best vehicle for earnest and profound communication of significant ethical and religious views.

THE VOICE OF WISDOM

A Greek of the fifth century would, of course, have felt very differently about the matter. He would not have objected at all to the presence of morality, didacticism [moral teachings], even "messages" in poetry, and especially the drama. Indeed, he felt that moral instruction was a vital and valuable function of tragic drama, in particular, and that the voice of the poet was the voice of morality and wisdom as well as of beauty. Indeed, it was an habitual tendency of the Greek mind to identify beauty and good, or rather to accept this identification without any question (in any dictionary of ancient Greek, the adjective *kalos* will be translated as "beautiful, good, genuine, virtuous, noble, honorable"; its opposite, *kakos*, as "ugly, cowardly, base, bad, evil"). This attitude is clearly reflected in the fifth-century view toward any form of art; that which is beautiful must be morally good, and that which is evil must of necessity also be ugly. Aesthetic pleasure and moral instruction are truly one and inseparable, a unity soon to be recognized by Aristotle in his recurrent emphasis on the moral character of the kind of agents fitted for tragic drama, and in the more ethical aspects of his *catharsis* [cleansing the emotions while viewing a tragedy]. To sum up, the Greeks of the fifth century and well into the fourth were convinced that poetry, especially tragedy, is essentially moral; that there is meaning in the drama, and that meaning is closely related to the aesthetic impact of the whole. Thus, to the contemporaries of Sophocles, a poet was expected to express a view of life, even a "message." Had he not done so, he would have failed his audiences. Had they thought he had not done so, he would not have won prizes in the Theater of Dionysos. But did Sophocles truly play the game within the rules established by his cultural tradition? Did he instruct as well as delight, adorn charm with wisdom? Do the tragedies embody an earnest view of life, or are they only exciting and superbly devised re-enactments of impossible situations, designed to absorb our emotions for a couple of hours, and send us out the aisles in some kind of limp and exhausted state of purification?

MORALISTS VERSUS FORMALISTS

Agreement on this issue, in our time, appears to be out of reach; the spectrum of Sophoclean criticism has broadened noticeably in recent years. Let C.M. Bowra [author of *Sophoclean Tragedy*] speak for the moralists:

> The central idea of a Sophoclean tragedy is that through suffering a man learns to be modest before the gods.... When [the characters] are finally forced to see the truth, we know that the gods have prevailed and that men must accept their own insignificance.

In short, for Bowra, the essence of each play of Sophocles is a message urging humility and piety. The poet wants to teach us something important, and he does it effectively.

For the formalists, A.J.A. Waldock [author of *Sophocles the Dramatist*] answers the moralists with appealing indignation, in his discussion of the Oedipus Tyrannus:

> We know little of Sophocles' religion. When we sum up what we know of his beliefs we find them meagre in number and depressingly commonplace in quality.... He believed that there are ups and downs in fortune, and that men are never secure.... There is religion in the *Oedipus Tyrannus*, but it is not all crucial in the drama.... *There is no meaning in the Oedipus Tyrannus* [italics mine]. There is merely the terror of coincidence, and then, at the end of it all, our impression of man's power to suffer, and of his greatness because of this power.

Now Waldock's reaction is surely a needed response to the ultramoralistic notion that Sophocles was driven by an urge to warn his contemporaries that they should not be rash or proud lest a vengeful heaven strike them down, and eager to communicate this unusual advice, set it in open code in the story of Oedipus. But as so often, reaction becomes overreaction; it is hard to believe, with the extreme formalist, that the playwright was little interested in attitudes and values, but only in dramatic or even theatrical display; that any meaning is ... coincidental to brilliance of structure, and without organic relationship to form. What sensitive audience could view the *Oedipus Tyrannus* and leave the theater not wondering why this man had to suffer what he suffered, and why the gods played the role they unquestionably played? ... In fact, to accept the formalist attitude without qualification is to accuse Sophocles of a serious artistic blunder—he has *compelled* his audience to absorb itself in ethical and spiritual considerations that have little or nothing to do with his genuine dramatic aims! He has diverted the attention of the viewer from dramatic form and power to unintended commonplaces.

To return to Waldock. He regards the *Tyrannus*, produced perhaps in 428, as a superb exercise in structure, a moving masterpiece of theater, an intricate piece of machinery designed to startle, dazzle, and shock. . . . But as having no serious meaning.

NOT ENOUGH STUFF FOR A PLAY?

Some twenty-two years later, Sophocles died, just having written his last play, *Oedipus at Colonus*. Was this another experiment in structural virtuosity [mastery], without any hard center of meaning? To a degree, says Waldock; now the old Sophocles, attracted by the theme of the death of Oedipus . . . was faced with the necessity of stretching out, with dramatic or near-melodramatic tensions, a story that did not really contain enough stuff for a play. . . . The scholar's argument seems reasonable. If it is right, we must conclude that much of the *Oedipus at Colonus* is compelling theater, but not highly serious, organically unified drama.

An amusing myth has invaded and established itself in certain areas of the academic world: that Sophocles composed a Theban *trilogy; Oedipus Tyrannus, Oedipus at Colonus*, and *Antigone*. This despite the odd fact that the production of the third preceded the first by about thirteen years, that the second followed the first by about twenty-two, and that the problems of the *Antigone* are in many ways so alien to those of the later plays. I suspect that the intrusion of the myth has persuaded many teachers besides myself to raise a storm warning for our students: "beware of interpreting any one of the Theban plays in terms of another." This signal of danger is surely soundly displayed. But in the case of the two Oedipus plays, the warning may lead to excessive caution. While a much older Sophocles wrote the *Oedipus at Colonus*, it was surely a Sophocles who recalled vividly the dramatic problems he had struggled with in the *Oedipus Tyrannus*, and who might well expect the mature element of his audience to remember the form and impact of the earlier play.

A comparison of the structure of the two later Theban plays strongly suggests that this supposition is accurate. To a startling degree, the *Oedipus at Colonus* seems to mirror the formal design of the *Oedipus Tyrannus*, and to reverse it in mirror fashion. In the *O.T.* [*Oedipus Tyrannus*], Oedipus is seen at the outset as fully endowed with the sight of reason, mature, admired, independent of others, while others are wholly dependent on him; in the *O.C.* [*Oedipus at Colonus*], he is blind, helpless, abominated, reliant on a girl, Antigone. In the former, he has the power to curse the unknown criminal, and is thus nearly divine (confident of Apollo's will), sure of his strength and foresight; in the latter, he must abjectly pray to the Eumenides [divine forces] for guidance and help. Next, in the *O.T.*, he is the self-assured king in search of the murderer of Laius, and after that, in quest of his own identity. In the *O.C.*, he is the quarry of a quest by others, by Creon and Polyneices, who no more know him for what he is, than he knew the unknown assassin, in the earlier play, for what (or who) he was then. Oedipus did not understand the power of the forces he confronted in the *O.T.*, while Creon and Polyneices show no real comprehension of the power now embodied in the old blind man whom they hope to enlist in their services. The physical blinding of the king in the earlier play coincides with the awakening of his spiritual vision into reality, and he turns to reliance on his daughter and his stick; in the *O.C.*, the old beggar . . . gently pushes his daughter Antigone aside, and with his eyes opened to fuller reality, leads Theseus to the holy place where no others can follow. Finally, at the end of the *O.T.*, he enters the palace, the proper secular dominion in which his birthright lay. But in the *O.C.*, he is mysteriously accepted into the grove of the Eumenides, his sacred birthright, and transfigured by the extraordinary powers of the earth, here to be granted the sanctified and universal hospitality which Sophocles thought the reward of the exceptional sufferer. And for the poet, the exceptional sufferer is man.

Structure and Thought Inseparable

The riddle of the Sphinx [that a person crawls on all fours as an infant, walks on two feet as an adult, and uses a cane in old age] is close to the heart of both plays. In the *O.T.*, Oedipus re-enacts the riddle; as infant on the slopes of [Mount] Kithaeron, as the kind and intelligent king at the beginning of the tragedy, as the faltering blind man at the end. The *O.C.* reverses this motif as well. Decrepit helplessness in the opening scenes, the flash-back to infancy, the assured domination and confidence at the end. . . . It is . . . tempting to suppose that the much older Sophocles, knowing that burial would soon unite him with his fellow-townsman, Oedipus [Sophocles was born at Colonus, the setting of the play], looked back to the *Tyrannus* and found it wanting—but in meaning, not structure. It had presented a solution to the Sphinx's riddle, had offered as answer a definition of man. But that definition had been two-dimensional . . . the magnificence of reason, and mortal frailty. The lacking third dimension is projected, largely by structure, in the final play. It resides in the mystically felt and logically undemonstrable spiritual transcendancy of man, the quintessence [purest qualities] of his being, not to be found in his confident rationality or in the magnitude of his suffering. . . .

By the conscious reversal of structure in the *Oedipus at Colonus*, Sophocles shows us that he was not merely playing a clever formal game, or creating virtuoso variations on a theme of his earlier years. Rather the structural inversion points to a deep rethinking of serious ethical, even metaphysical attitudes. As critics we may not share those attitudes, we may possibly think them shallow, we may find them to be not much more than commonplaces of the Athenian tradition. But however we may evaluate his thought, we have no license to dismiss it as unintended or inconsequential to the emotive effect of his theater. Structure and thought are inseparable in the seven [surviving Sophoclean] plays; to stress one element and disregard the other is a decision of Solomon, a dismemberment [tearing apart] of the living work of art.

Comparing Sophocles to Aeschylus

Edith Hamilton

In this excerpt from her famous and highly ac-
claimed book *The Greek Way to Western Civilization*,
Edith Hamilton, one of the most eloquent of
twentieth-century classical scholars, compares
Sophocles' gifts and style to those of his older contemporary, Aeschylus. Citing brief examples from
their respective works, Hamilton makes the point that
Sophocles' plots and speeches were almost always
simply constructed, direct, cool, clear, and most of all
unadorned by excessive description and emotion; by
contrast, she maintains, Aeschylus was an unre-
strained romantic, a master of color, deep shading,
and dramatic power. Aeschylus may have been the
grander dramatist, Hamilton suggests, but Sophocles
was Greek theater's most perfect workman.

In every way Sophocles is the embodiment of what we know
as Greek, so much so that all definitions of the Greek spirit
and Greek art are first of all definitions of his spirit and his
art. He has imposed himself upon the world as the quintes-
sential Greek, and the qualities preeminently his are as-
cribed to all the rest. He is direct, lucid, simple, reasonable.
Excess—the word is not to be mentioned in his presence.
Restraint is his as no other writer's. Beauty to him does not
inhere in color, or light and shade, or any method of adorn-
ment, but in structure, in line and proportion, or, from another point of view, it has its roots not in mystery but in clear
truthfulness. This is the classic spirit as we have conceived
it, and contrasted with Sophocles, Aeschylus is a romanti-
cist. How sober is Sophocles' utterance even in despair. His
most desperate sayings have an air of reasonableness:

> Only the base will long for length of life
> that never turns another way from evil.

> What joy is there in day that follows day,
> now swift, now slow, and death the only goal.
> I count as nothing him who feels within
> the glow of empty hopes.

And how romantic is Aeschylus' despair:

> Black smoke I would be
> nearing the clouds of God.
> All unseen, soaring aloft,
> as dust without wings I would perish.
> Oh, for a seat high in air,
> where the dripping clouds turn snow,
> a sheer, bare cliff, outranging sight,
> brooding alone, aloft.
> Down I would hurl myself, deep down,
> and only the eagles would see.

The last words spoken by the two Antigones bring into clear relief the difference between the two men's temperaments. Sophocles' Antigone mourns:

> Unwept, unfriended, without marriage song,
> I pass on my last journey to my grave.
> Behold me, what I suffer and from whom,
> because I have upheld that which is high.

Not so Aeschylus' heroine:

> No one shall ever thus decree for me.
> I am a woman and yet will I make
> a grave, a burying for him ... With my own hands!
> Courage! For I will find the power to act.
> Speak not to stay me.

A TENDER AND GENTLE SPIRIT

Aristophanes [the Greek comic playwright] in the *Frogs* gives a sketch of Sophocles which is in singular contrast to the mocking portraits of everybody else. The rest brawl like fishwives and fight like bad little boys, Aeschylus and Euripides foremost. Sophocles stands aloof, gentle and courteous and ready to give place to others, "blameless in life and blameless, too, in death." Not even Aristophanes could then jeer at Sophocles to an Athenian audience. There is no other proof so convincing of the general level of intelligence and cultivated understanding in Athens as the fact that Sophocles was the popular playwright. But however great and sad the difference between the taste of the theatre public then and now, in one respect they are the same: general popularity always means warmth of human sympathy. In Sophocles' plays one may catch a glimpse here and there of that tender and gentle spirit which so endeared him to the Athenians, and which is moving as only the tenderness and the gentleness of the very strong can be. The blinded Oedipus begging for his children:

> Let me touch them—Oh, could I but touch them with my hands, I would think that they were with me as when once I could behold them. Do I hear weeping? My beloved near me? Come to me, my children. Come here to my hands.

That is a new note. There is nothing like it in Aeschylus. . . .

The supreme excellence of both men is the same. Alas for us, that it is one which for Sophocles was lost in its complete perfection when classic Greek ceased to be a spoken language. A great thought can live forever, passed on from tongue to tongue, but a great style lives only in one language. Of all English poets [John] Milton is least read by non-English-speaking people. Shakespeare may almost be called German as well as English, but Milton is English alone. Sophocles and Milton are the two incomparable stylists. They are always artists of the great style. They maintain a continuous level of loveliness of word, of phrase, of musical sweep and pause. Compared to them Aeschylus and Shakespeare are faulty workmen, capable of supreme felicity of expression side by side with grotesque distortion. Milton's poetry is typically English in its genius; it is poetry of magnificent opulence, of weighted phrase and gorgeous adjective, but there are times when he becomes so limpid, simple, clear, direct, that he is classic, and for one who cannot read Greek easily the surest way to catch a glimpse of that flawless perfection of utterance which is Sophocles, is to read Milton:

> Sabrina fair,
> Listen where thou art sitting
> Under the glassy, cool, translucent wave . . .
> While the still morn went out with sandals gray. . . .

That is the way Sophocles can write.

And completely Sophoclean in substance and in style is:

> Come, come; no time for lamentations now,
> Nor much more cause. Samson hath quit himself
> Like Samson and heroicly hath finished
> A life heroic. . . .
> Nothing is here for tears, nothing to wail
> Or knock the breast, no weakness, no contempt,
> Dispraise or blame; nothing but well and fair,
> And what may calm us in a death so noble.

It is hard to believe that Sophocles did not write that.

A GREATER POET THAN A DRAMATIST?

Milton was no dramatist. Thought was his great interest, not action. Sophocles turned naturally to the drama. He was a man of Periclean Athens where preeminently the play was the thing, but it is open to question whether his own bent would have led him that way. It is certain that he is a greater poet than dramatist. In dramatic power he stands below Aeschylus. On the other hand, in good theatre, as distinguished from sheer drama, he is his superior, but that is only to say that he possessed in the highest degree the Athenian technical gift: in whatever direction he turned he was a consummate workman. If he wrote a play it would be done as well as it could be done from every point of view of theatrical craftsmanship. One imagines the young man watching a performance of Aeschylus' *Libation-Bearers* and noting every crude detail and the passing over of many a chance for a tense moment: that lock of Orestes' hair they will never have done talking about; the patent silliness of Electra's divining that her brother has arrived because the foot-prints she has found are like her own; the scene where she recognizes him, so quickly passed over when it held most admirable dramatic possibilities. And off he goes to do a really well-made play. Such is the *Electra*. So brief, but not a word wasted; Electra's character given in a moment by the sharp contrast to her sister; the intense, compressed dialogue, where every word means something different to the speakers and the spectators, and the effect is electric; that lock of hair relegated far to the background; the recognition scene worked to the full of all its possibilities; and in the end a thrilling moment. The son [Orestes] has come to avenge his father's death at the hands of his wife [Clytemnestra] and her lover [Aegisthus] by murdering the two murderers. He has killed his mother, having gained admission to her by declaring that he is bringing her news of his own death. His sister [Electra] waits at the palace door. To her comes their mother's lover, rejoicing that the one man they feared is dead:

AEGISTHUS: Where are the strangers who have brought us news of Orestes slain?

ELECTRA: Within. They have found a way to the heart of their hostess.

AEGISTHUS: Can I look upon the corpse with my own eyes?

ELECTRA: You can indeed.

[*The palace doors open. The shrouded corpse of* CLYTEMNESTRA *lies just within.* ORESTES *stands over it.*]

AEGISTHUS: Uncover the face that I, who was his kinsman, may pay my due tribute of mourning.

ORESTES: Do you yourself lift the veil.

AEGISTHUS: So be it—but you, Electra, call me Clytemnestra if she is near.

ORESTES: She is. Look no farther for her.

[AEGISTHUS *lifts the face cloth.*]

AEGISTHUS: What do I see—

ORESTES: Why so terrified? Is the face strange to you?

The lifting of that cloth is a supreme theatrical touch. It is the great moment in the play. But the story Sophocles was dramatizing centered around a situation which could not be surpassed for dramatic opportunity, the murder of a mother by her son. No attention is focused on this fact in the play. When the son comes out after killing his mother, he and his sister agree briefly that it is well done, and turn instantly to the real climax, the killing of Aegisthus. Sophocles deliberately avoided the horror of that first murder. He substituted for it the righteous punishment of a murderer, a death that could move no one to pity and awe. "Thoughts too great for man," he ever held, are not for man to utter. He had the sure instinct of the consummate artist: what was too tremendous ever to be done in finished perfection he would not attempt. The high passion that is needed for the very highest drama was not in him. He had a supreme gift of poetic expression, a great intellect, and an unsurpassed sureness of beautiful workmanship, but he did not rise to the heights where Aeschylus and Shakespeare alone have walked.

How Sophocles Viewed and Portrayed the Gods

Herbert J. Muller

Former Cornell and Purdue Universities professor Herbert J. Muller, in his widely read and authoritative book *The Spirit of Tragedy*, points out that no one knows for sure how strongly Sophocles believed in the gods, or, for that matter, whether he believed in them at all. Yet his plays are replete with references to these deities, some honoring them, others expressing fear or awe of them, and still others accepting that human beings must inevitably face their divine judgment. Thus, whatever his personal views, Muller argues, Sophocles clearly recognized the important role the gods played in Greek society and the expectations his theater audiences had about his characters' interactions with these deities. Ultimately though, says Muller, the playwright's own faith seems to present the idea that people, though mortal, have within them a divine spark and certain potential heroic traits not unlike those of the gods themselves. And his greatest characters are those who, in the face of horrendous and crushing hardships, display courage, dignity, resolve, and honor.

The traditional view of Sophocles is ... one to induce an awed hush, and some suspicion. The ancients called him "the most god-fearing of mankind," and the most serene and blessed in his life. For later ages he became the classical example of *sophrosyne*, the virtue of self-restraint. He is also considered the supreme artist of Greek tragedy, representing the apex of its development. "When a critic can improve a play of Sophocles," writes [historian H.D.F.] Kitto, "he may be sure that he is only giving it a turn that Sophocles had already rejected." In the last century the admiration of his

From *The Spirit of Tragedy* by Herbert J. Muller. Copyright ©1956 by Herbert J. Muller. Reprinted by permission of Alfred A. Knopf, Inc.

artistry was intensified by the discovery of Sophoclean irony, which gave currency to the terms "dramatic" or "tragic" irony, and the "irony of fate." Nevertheless classicists continued to stress his famous piety. . . .

[For example, in *Oedipus at Colonus,* he has the chorus say]

> Now let the weeping cease;
> Let no one mourn again.
> These things are in the hands of God.

. . . These things remain a mystery. The lines recall the pious, god-fearing Sophocles of tradition, but who is this God? What are his purposes for man? Sophocles does not say. His plays as a whole give a surprisingly vague, confused impression of the nature of the gods he feared. . . .

What were the views of Sophocles about man and the gods, the meaning of man's life? Given the diversity of his plays, his refusal to be explicit, and the basic disagreements among his admirers, it would be impertinent to declare that the answer is clear or certain. Some would say that the very question is impertinent. Professor [A.J.A.] Waldock [author of the 1951 book *Sophocles the Dramatist*], who writes with refreshing good sense about the plays and their problems, objects to the notion that great plays must contain profound truths, or even "mean something"; to him *Oedipus Rex* is simply a wonderful story, about a highly exceptional rather than a universal situation. The whole uncertainty about the "meaning" of these plays would seem to indicate that their greatness does not depend on any specific meaning. Yet Sophocles was manifestly a thoughtful writer, concerned with major issues of human conduct and human destiny. Almost all readers feel that his plays positively do "mean something"—that he was expressing, however obliquely, some "philosophy of life." And almost all commentators agree on certain qualities that are clues to his thought, notably his irony and his refusal to declare himself in so many words. In our own world these might imply a devotion to art for art's sake. In the Greek world they imply a measure of philosophical skepticism. Sophocles was at least saying that the ways of deity [the gods] are mysterious, and often painfully so.

THE POWERS THAT RULE THE UNIVERSE

This does not mean that he was an atheist, or even an agnostic in the modern sense. Since we are always prone to

ORESTES REVEALS HIMSELF TO ELECTRA

In this excerpt from Electra, *the title character's display of courage after hearing and believing the false news of the death of her brother, Orestes, is rewarded. As she stands holding an urn she thinks contains his ashes, Orestes confronts and then reveals himself to her.*

ORESTES. Is this the form of the illustrious Electra that I behold?

ELECTRA. It is; and very grievous in her plight.

ORESTES. Alas, then, for this miserable fortune!

ELECTRA. Surely, sir, your lament is not for *me?*

ORESTES. O form cruelly, godlessly, misused!

ELECTRA. Those ill-omened words, sir, fit no one better than me.

ORESTES. Alas for your life, unwedded and all unblest!

ELECTRA. Why this steadfast gaze, stranger, and these laments? . . .

ORESTES. Give up this urn, then, and you shall be told all.

ELECTRA. I beseech you, sir, do not be so cruel to me!

ORESTES. Do as I say, and never fear to do amiss.

ELECTRA. I conjure you, do not rob me of my chief treasure!

ORESTES. You must not keep it.

ELECTRA. Ah woe is me for you, Orestes, if I am not to give you burial!

ORESTES. Hush! No such word! You have no right to lament.

ELECTRA. No right to lament for my dead brother?

ORESTES. It is not proper for you to speak of him so. . . .

ELECTRA. And where is that unhappy one's tomb?

ORESTES. There is none; the living have no tomb.

ELECTRA. What are you saying, boy?

ORESTES. Nothing that is not true.

ELECTRA. The man is alive?

ORESTES. If there is life in me.

ELECTRA. What? Are you he?

ORESTES. Look at this signet, once our father's, and judge if I speak truth.

ELECTRA. O blissful day!

ORESTES. Blissful in very deed!

ELECTRA. Is this your voice?

ORESTES. Let no other voice reply.

ELECTRA. Do I hold you in my arms?

ORESTES. As you may hold me always!

ELECTRA. Ah, dear friends and fellow-citizens, behold Orestes here, who was feigned dead, and now by that feigning has come safely home!

read our own attitudes into our favorite authors of the past, equip them with all the conveniences of modern thought, it should be stressed that the skepticism of Sophocles was fundamentally different from most contemporary skepticism. Nowhere in the plays is there a suggestion that he doubted the *existence* of the gods. All the plays testify to their power, all give a sense of a sovereign order above mere chance or happenstance. The very point of the most outrageous coincidences, as in the fate of Oedipus, is that they are not accidental but preordained; they were foretold by oracles—and the oracles are invariably right in Sophocles. Nor is there in *Oedipus Rex* the deep sense of outrage that modern readers may feel. None of the characters, including the Chorus, complains that Thebans are suffering for no fault of their own, in this plague sent by the gods; they simply assume that Thebes must be properly purified of its defilement. Although technically innocent, Oedipus accepts his "guilt": he is the defiled one, and must make amends. Like most Greeks, Sophocles apparently took for granted that innocent and guilty must suffer alike when the gods punish. While troubled by such divine injustice, he does not make an indignant issue of it. He was never so severe a critic of the Olympians [a reference to the gods residing atop Mount Olympus] as Euripides was.

Both gods and oracles might have been mere symbols for Sophocles, or dramatic conveniences. Yet they were evidently real to him, in a sense hard for us to understand and impossible to define exactly. What can we make of the apparently authentic report that when the new cult of Asclepius [a famous healer] came to Athens, Sophocles entertained the god in his own home while a suitable shrine was being prepared? We cannot imagine Euripides inviting a god to his home—or Aeschylus either, for that matter. We might say conscientiously that Sophocles was hospitable because he was public-minded and open-minded, or skeptical of his own skepticism, but we really feel that he was strangely naive. We can hope to understand his apparent superstition only if we keep in mind a basic assumption that very few Greeks [of his time] questioned . . . the assumption that the powers that rule the universe, whoever or whatever they be, are not indifferent to man. For better or worse, these powers are concerned with his fate.

But the tragic fact remains that it might be for worse, for no intelligible reason. Given the assumption of a supernatural order, the crucial questions are: What is its relation to man? What are its purposes? The answer of Sophocles is in effect that its purposes are inscrutable [mysterious]. His plays do not represent the rule of the gods as always reasonable, just, and beneficent, but neither do they represent it as merely unreasonable or unjust. In the face of the ultimate mystery he could entertain different possibilities—or more simply, might express different moods. *Oedipus Rex* reflects a pessimism that in *Women of Trachis* approaches despair; *Philoctetes* and *Oedipus at Colonus* suggest a pious acceptance that approaches serenity. From his work as a whole, however, what comes through to us unmistakably is neither pessimism nor piety but the deep sense of mystery that underlies both.

One sign of this is his distinctive irony. In Sophocles irony is more than the dramatic device that Aeschylus had learned to employ, and that Aristotle discussed under the labels of Discoveries, Reversals, etc. It becomes a way of viewing life that most clearly distinguishes him from Aeschylus, and that Aristotle ignored. It is a philosophical perception of "the irony of fate": an awareness that heroes are by their nature built for ruin, and that their fate is incongruous, "wrong," but also in some sense appropriate, in any case natural. It is an awareness that the tragic situation . . . is primary and uncaused, a condition rather than an act—the condition that Oedipus was born into. . . .

THE HEROIC SPIRIT

Nevertheless ironic detachment is a way of viewing life, not a sufficient way of living—at least in the Greek *polis* for which Sophocles wrote, and to which he was devoted. It brings up a further question: how should man bear himself under so mysterious and hard a dispensation? Again Sophocles gives no one definite answer. He evidently respected the conventional wisdom of resignation [giving in to fate] so often expressed by his choruses. Pride may aggravate the woes of man, who is not the measure of all things; patience, piety, and purity may help him to endure. Yet the heroes of Sophocles live by a different code. If they must be proud and willful in order to be protagonists of tragedy, he treats them with a more evident respect. He does not plainly condemn their pride unless, as in the Creon of *Antigone*, it is purely selfish or tyrannical. He creates timid foils for Antigone and

Electra to set off their heroic spirit, or "noble excess." Among the functions of his choruses is an ironic role, for by their typical counsel of "Play it safe" they too set off this noble excess. Most of all, it seems to me, Sophocles honors the heroic spirit.

Thus Ajax in his unendurable shame surrenders only his life. He will not "huddle over the coals of flickering hope"; deprived of honor in life, he will still have it in death. He denies flatly that he now owes "any duty or service" to the gods. His dying prayer is not for forgiveness but for the punishment of his enemies. The Chorus remarks that he died as he had lived, "a willful man"; and the rest of the play is a tribute to him. In *Electra* the climax is another revelation of the heroic spirit. The report of the death of Orestes provides an ironic cross-scene, as Clytemnestra rejoices, Electra despairs, and the audience knows that the news is false; but it is also the crucial test of Electra's courage, since Orestes has represented her one hope of freedom and revenge. She meets the test by resolving to carry out her duty anyway. . . . And most emphatic is the vindication of Oedipus in *Oedipus at Colonus*. The gods, we are told, have given him grace; but what the play shows is a proud king defending his past, maintaining his own ways, earning his apotheosis [attainment of glory or divine status] by integrity and strength of mind. We are not given to see the gods who receive him, but only the god-like element in Oedipus himself.

Cedric Whitman [author of the 1951 book *Sophocles: A Study of Heroic Humanism*], one of the few critics to stress the humanism instead of the god-fearing piety of Sophocles, was inspired by the apotheosis of Oedipus to assert that "for sheer audacity and defiant insistence on human dignity, this vision of 'divine man' puts to shame all doctrines of the soul's immortality." Sophocles would probably have thought this language too proud, as well as a little strange; his vision seems no more audacious or defiant than Homer's, and somewhat sadder. Yet he was in the Homeric tradition, where ancient critics placed him. If he seems to have had more reverence for the gods than Homer had, and perhaps more fear, he had the same respect for the heroic spirit, the excellence that man can attain by his own efforts. The religious belief remains uncertain; the belief in human dignity is all the clearer for such uncertainty. This humanistic faith, I should say, was the soul of his art.

In Sophoclean Tra{
Humans Create Th{
Own Fate

Frank B. Jevons

One of the most often discussed themes of tragedy,
especially ancient Greek tragedy, is fatalism, the idea
or belief that human actions are largely guided by the
unseen hand of fate, destiny, the gods, or perhaps
some other outside or supernatural force. As the distinguished scholar Frank B. Jevons, a former professor at England's University of Durham, explains, the
element of fate threads its way through the background of most of the works of Aeschylus and Sophocles. The difference in their approaches, he points out,
is that Aeschylus made his human characters seem
like puppets of the gods, whereas Sophocles made his
characters responsible for their own actions. Thus, in
Sophoclean drama the gods warn people not to do a
certain thing and if they do it anyway they themselves
must shoulder the blame. This leads Jevons into a discussion of the way Sophocles highlighted and explored the irony of some of the situations in which his
characters find themselves. A situation they see as
productive or innocent is in reality destructive and
dangerous, not because the gods fated it to be that
way, but because of the characters' own shortcomings.

By bringing down philosophy from the skies to the earth,
Socrates gave a new direction to philosophy, which philosophy has retained to this day. In a different sense, Sophocles
brought down the drama from the skies to the earth, and the
drama still follows the course which Sophocles first marked
out for it. It was on the gods, the struggles of the gods, and on
destiny that Aeschylus dwelt; it is with man that Sophocles is
concerned. From this difference flow all the differences be-

From Frank B. Jevons, *A History of Greek Literature: From the Earliest Period to the
Death of Demosthenes* (London: Charles Griffin, 1886).

tween the two poets, and herein consists the advance which Sophocles made in the development of the drama. Such action as the plays of Aeschylus possess they derive from the force of destiny. What is done by a character in the Aeschylean drama is, it is true, consistent with that character. The murder of Agamemnon [in Aeschylus's *Oresteia*] could be expected from Clytemnestra alone. But although she is suited to the deed and the deed to her, if we ask *why* she murdered Agamemnon, we shall find that the reason lies, not in her character nor in her circumstances but, in her destiny. . . . Clytemnestra herself says it was not she who killed Agamemnon, but the evil "destiny of the Atridae" taking her form. In Sophocles, on the other hand, the motive force of the drama is always to be found in the passions of men, and not in the external action of destiny. The Ajax of Sophocles commits suicide, not because he is fated to do so, but because to him, after his disgrace, life is not merely distasteful, but impossible. The force at work here is internal, and consists in the feelings of Ajax. On the contrary, the Orestes of Aeschylus has no proper motion of his own. He is simply the channel through which the action of the gods flows. What he does is not his own doing, but what Apollo bids. The force is from without, not from within. Contrast this with Sophocles. Every action of Oedipus is the natural necessary outcome of his character and his circumstances, and when peace does come to him, it is from within. . . . In Aeschylus we have symbolism, in Sophocles poetic truth.

NO COMPLAINT WITH THE GODS

Although, in Sophocles, the mainspring of man's actions is men's passions, we still find fatalism [belief in fate] in Sophocles, but not the fatalism of Aeschylus. With Aeschylus, Atreus commits a crime, and the punishment falls upon his children for generations in the shape of a destiny compelling them to crimes. With Sophocles, the house of the Labdacidae is indeed under a similar curse, but the cause of Oedipus' deeds is not destiny, but circumstances and himself. The fatalism of Sophocles is that of Herodotus [the Greek historian], and probably of the ordinary Greek of the time. It may be illustrated from Herodotus. According to the historian, Croesus, the father of Atys, learning from an oracle that his son was destined to perish by an iron weapon, confined him to the house with the purpose of evading the doom foretold by the oracle. The son, however, persuaded Croesus to allow him to go to the chase, and then was accidentally killed by the very person to whose care Croesus, in his dread of the oracle, had intrusted him. This is the worst kind of fatalism, for it teaches that man cannot avoid his fate, whatever he may do, and thus encourages helpless . . . resignation to an imaginary necessity. This was the fatalism which Sophocles found and accepted. But if he adopted this and other common beliefs, he, as a poet, by adopting them elevated and refined them.

It is probably impossible to discuss Sophocles' attitude towards fatalism without reading into him at least some ideas which could not be present to the mind of any Greek. It is difficult to always realise that Sophocles knew nothing of the free-will controversy, and consequently felt no alarm at fatalism. Remembering, however, this fact, we shall not consider it a paradox to say that Sophocles shows how men run on their fate of their own free-will. Oedipus is warned by Apollo of his doom, and he fulfils his doom; but all his acts are his own; neither man nor God can be blamed. The lesson as well as the art of Sophocles is that man's fate, though determined by the gods, depends on his actions, and his actions on himself and his circumstances. The contradiction which to us is involved in this did not exist for Sophocles. If Sophocles did not find out any incompatibility between free-will and fatalism, neither did he see in fatalism any imputation on [fault or corruption with] the justice of the gods. Indeed, the contrary is the case. . . . In him we find no complaint of the injustice of the gods. On the contrary, the gods warn man, and yet man does what they have tried to save him from. The heavens speak to man, but he understands them not. If Oedipus is not to be blamed, neither certainly are the gods. For Sophocles, fatalism was consistent both with free-will and with the justice of the gods; on neither subject had he any doubts to solve. Nor does his tragedy concern itself to give an answer to the question, why do the innocent suffer? The innocent *do* suffer, and that fact is the tragedy of life. His plays are not works of theology; their object is not to solve problems. The sufferings of the innocent cause pity and fear, and thus serve in tragedy to redeem the crudity of fatalism. When Deianira [wife of Heracles in Sophocles' *The Women of Trachis*] in her love for her husband innocently causes his death, we feel the pity which it is the part of tragedy to excite; and when we read of Oedipus and his undeserved sufferings, we feel so much fear as is implied in obeying the utterance "Judge not."

THE IRONICAL MAN

In this connection we may consider the "irony of Sophocles." In argument irony has many forms. That which best illustrates the irony of Sophocles is the method by which the ironical man, putting apparently innocent questions or suggestions, leads some person from one preposterous statement to another, until, perhaps, the subject of the irony realises his situation and discovers that when he thought he was most brilliant or impressive, then he was really most absurd. . . .

When Oedipus was told by Apollo that he would kill his father and commit incest with his mother, he at once fled from his home at Corinth, and found his way to Thebes. There he married the queen, became king, was blest with children and a glorious reign. When the revelation comes, he looks back upon his life only to see that the flight from Corinth, which was to take him far from his parents, led him to meet and kill his father and to wed his mother; that the children in whom he thought himself blest are the fruit of incest, and that the glory of his reign was a revolting horror. . . .

For the full appreciation of the irony of Sophocles, and of its artistic value in heightening the interest of the drama, it must be remembered that whereas the torturing contrast between the condition of Oedipus, as he fancies it, and as it really is, is only discovered by Oedipus at the last moment, this contrast is perpetually present from the beginning to the spectator. The artistic value of this is double. In the first place, the spectator having known the real state of things from the first, has all along been in the state of mind in which Oedipus finds himself when the revelation has come; and the consequence is that the spectator needs no explanation from Oedipus of his state of mind, but comprehends and sympathises at once with Oedipus when he blinds himself. Thus the action of the drama is enabled to proceed with a directness and rapidity which would be impossible if Oedipus had to explain the motives of his self-mutilation. In the second place, the contrast between Oedipus' fancied height of glory and his really piteous position is present to the mind of the spectator throughout. Thus every word in the drama has a doubled effect upon the feelings.

Sophocles' Invention of the Third Actor Widened the Scope of Drama

H.D.F. Kitto

Before Sophocles began writing plays, all of the speaking characters in Greek dramas (with the exception of the chorus members) were portrayed by two actors who changed masks during the course of the action in order to assume different identities. Obviously, under these circumstances it was impractical to feature more than a few characters in a play, which limited the scope and complexity of the storytelling. In introducing the theatrical device of the third actor, Sophocles opened up possibilities for more complicated and varied interactions between characters and thereby increased the scope of the drama. In this excerpt from his well-known literary study of Greek tragedy, the renowned classical historian H.D.F. Kitto explores some of the ways that Sophocles used the third actor in *Oedipus Tyrannus*, *Antigone*, *Ajax*, and *Philoctetes*. The reader need not have read these plays or know the plots to follow Kitto's analysis, for in each instance he makes basically the same point—that these various combinations of characters and the ways they advance their respective stories would be impossible without the presence of a third actor, whether in the role of a messenger, a watchman, or some other character.

Why did Sophocles [introduce the theatrical device of the third actor?] ... Although the first twenty years of his dramatic activity are practically a blank, we can answer the question with some confidence: he wanted the third actor in order to do what Aeschylus resolutely refuses to do with him in the *Agamemnon*, namely to illuminate the chief character

Excerpted from H.D.F. Kitto, *Greek Tragedy: A Literary Study*, 3rd edition (London: Methuen, 1966). Reprinted with permission of the publisher.

from several points of view. . . . Sophocles sees not the simplicities but the complexities of life. Certain persons, because they are like this and not like that, and because their circumstances are these and not those, combine to bring about the catastrophe. Had any detail been different the disaster would not have occurred. The working of Law is seen in the way in which all these delicate complexities dovetail, to make a pattern which is suddenly seen to be inevitable.

The Sophoclean hero, because he is complex, not single-minded, must be seen from more than one point of view. We do not know our Creon or our Oedipus, we cannot therefore understand his tragedy, until we have seen how he behaves to a diversity of people and (equally important) how they behave to him. Oedipus' consideration for his people, his courtesy to Creon and Teiresias which quickly passes to suspicion and rage, Creon's attitude to Haemon—these are not decorations or improvements; it is essential to the tragedy that we should know our heroes like this. Similarly the Watchman's reluctance to face Creon is important as a sidelight on the King's character, not only sub-comic relief. Eteocles' colourless Spy is transformed, necessarily, into this attractive character of flesh and blood. This is not 'progress'; it is plain logic. This art of 'undercutting' is used in the [*Oedipus*] *Tyrannus* as it has rarely been used since, when the supreme eminence of Oedipus is shown by the collapse of Jocasta's bold scepticism.

Here, we may be sure, we have the origin of the third actor, but there was an accessory cause and a development. No catastrophe can be self-contained; others besides the sinner are involved. To Aeschylus this necessary aspect of tragedy presented itself as a linear movement, hence the trilogy; either the tragic event is the result of inherited character, or it leaves a legacy of tragedy for the next generation. To Sophocles this idea presents itself in a complexive way, as one immediate situation which involves others at once. Ajax' vanity ruins Ajax, but it endangers, too, his sailors, Tecmessa, Eurysaces, Teucer; Creon's stubbornness threatens the Watchman and destroys Antigone before, through Haemon and Eurydice, it involves Creon himself. Thus again more actors are wanted.

Further, if we may trust our scanty evidence, Sophocles began to lay more weight on the tragic interworking of circumstance with character, so that situation becomes more complex. In these four plays, as we shall see in a moment, there is a distinct 'improvement' in the manipulation of the three actors. The explanation is not that Sophocles is perfecting his technique, or not only this, but that his thought is taking a new direction. It is significant that as plot becomes more complex the hero's character becomes less catastrophic. Oedipus and Electra are very different from Ajax and Creon; we feel that these last are so ill-balanced that a slight push may upset them; the former are of such a nobility that only a most unlucky combination of circumstances can bring them low. So, against a more balanced characterization, we have a more complex situation, and the more complex situation brings the use of the three actors to its highest degree of fluidity.

AN IMAGINATIVE PIECE OF THEATER

Let us now consider this use in four plays. In the *Ajax* the third actor plays a restricted but significant part. Between the Prologue and the last scene his only effect on the piece is that he enables the not very dramatic Messenger to give his news to Tecmessa as well as to the chorus. The use of the third actor is restricted in this way because the plot is such that the two chief actors, Ajax and Odysseus, cannot meet. This explains why Sophocles, who had for twenty years been writing for three actors, makes little of them here.

The Prologue uses the three actors well. Athena and Odysseus give us, as it were, the common-sense attitude to Ajax' crime; they also give us a direct view of Odysseus which contrasts excellently with the uncomprehending way in which the Ajax-group always speak of him. But it gives more than this. It is an astonishingly imaginative piece of 'theatre'. It is assumed that Athena, who is invisible to Odysseus, is visible to the audience. Why? Nothing in the scene demands it, and if she is hidden, speaking from behind, 'like the voice of a brazen trumpet', we have the fine spectacle of Odysseus alone on the stage with his raving enemy—alone but for the presence of the unseen goddess.

In the last scene, too, there is imaginativeness. After Menelaus comes Agamemnon; the succession of scenes is perhaps a little lacking in subtlety, but not in point, for it makes clear that Teucer has against him not the whim of one leader only but something like public opinion, and that Teucer cannot find the grounds for overturning that opinion.

Now Odysseus, the arch-enemy, arrives, and while he prevails over Agamemnon with such magnanimity [generosity] and good sense, Teucer stands by silent, astonished at this support from this source. He thanks Odysseus worthily.... Nothing could more finely indicate the intellectual loneliness of Odysseus among these men, and the point depends on this, that Teucer was present and heard Odysseus' argument. He was silent not because the play was written in 450 and Sophocles had not yet learned how to make him talk, but because Sophocles had more dramatic imagination than some of his critics.

USE OF THE THIRD ACTOR IN THE *ANTIGONE*

The Prologue of the *Antigone* does not use three actors, but as it is a scene such as only three-actor tragedy would contrive we may consider it briefly. Like all prologues it outlines the situation; like all good ones it does also something much more important. As the prologue of the *Ajax* presented the situation from a point of view different from that assumed during the greater part of the play, so here the private, personal and feminine atmosphere contrasts sharply with the full light of publicity in which the action is to be played out. It is an admirable preparation for the jubilant hymn of triumph that follows it. The prologue of the *Electra* does the same thing: the practical and political considerations of the two men make an excellent foil [contrast] to the desolation and the personal sorrow of Electra....

Two other scenes in the *Antigone* demand consideration. The first, that between Creon, the Watchman and Antigone, is extremely dramatic, a foreshadowing of the triangular [three-character] scenes in the *Tyrannus*. The dramatic power arises from this, that each of the three characters has his private preoccupation, his own attitude to the central fact. Creon is faced with the incredible news that the rebel is no political agent but his own niece; Antigone, the deed now done, stands apart, out of touch with the scene, rapt in her almost mystic confidence; the Watchman, finding in the situation his own vindication and escape, is completely at his ease, struck with the wonderfully irrelevant idea that a man should deny nothing—this is the moral that he draws.... He, a person on the outskirts of the tragedy, has escaped. That is how it affects him. It is only by an effort of ordinary decency that he can remember what it means to Antigone:

> ... partly to my joy, part to my pain.
> For to escape oneself from scathe is sweet,
> But sore it is to bring a friend to scathe.
> Yet nature bids me hold all else for cheap
> If so mine own deliverance I secure.

Once more, this is not dramatic decoration; it is the mocking way in which things do happen.

The second triangular scene of the *Antigone*, Creon-Antigone-Ismene, is not of such importance as the first. Both differ from Sophocles' later scenes of the kind in that the situation, though dramatic, does not develop; and this second scene is less significant than the earlier one, for Ismene does little to modify the situation or to heighten the tragedy. It illustrates Sophocles' methods rather than his philosophy. We saw Ismene in the prologue; it is the natural fulfilment of that if we see her again now, and are shown the effect on her of Antigone's deed. Her attitude in this second scene, an attitude of pure emotionalism, is indeed a foil to the clear and almost hard lines of Antigone's resolution, and Creon's utter bewilderment adds a dramatic point, but the significance is really structural; it is a link with the prologue and a preparation for the next theme—since Ismene is obviously the best person to introduce the matter of Antigone's betrothal to Haemon.

A COMBINATION OF CROSS-RHYTHMS

Coming to the two later plays we find an enormous advance in technique. In the two great discovery scenes of the *Tyrannus*, the situation is not presented practically complete before our eyes; not only does it grow, but it grows in opposite directions for the two chief actors. The conversation between Oedipus and the Corinthian Messenger is itself painfully dramatic, but the addition of Jocasta more than doubles the power of the scene. The progress of Jocasta from hope, through confidence, to frozen horror, and that of Oedipus from terror to a sublime resolution and assurance, the two connected by the commonplace cheerfulness of the Corinthian (who must be extremely puzzled by the tremendous effects his simple message is creating)—this makes as fine a combination of cross-rhythms as can well be imagined. Nor is the effect of the following scene inferior to this. Here it is Oedipus who ends in horror, while the direct contrast lies between the Corinthian, even more cheerful and helpful this time, and the Theban shepherd whose life-secret is being torn from him. There is nothing in dramatic literature to match the peculiar and awful beauty of these scenes except the passage in the *Electra* between the Paedagogus, Electra and Clytemnestra. The long and harsh wrangle between mother and daughter culminates in Clytemnestra's blasphemous petition to Apollo, and immediately, as if in answer to that prayer, the Paedagogus comes in with his statement of Orestes' death. Electra's answer is a cry of anguish; against this Clytemnestra's excitement, now as later, is finely drawn:

> What sayest thou, stranger? What? Do not listen to *her*!

Then comes the elaborate and vivid account of Orestes' supposed death: the most brilliant by far of Sophocles' speeches. . . . The speech is harsh; like the Crisean plain which it describes, it is strewn with wrecked chariots; the traditional limpidity [calm pleasantry] of Greek poetry is entirely missing. Exactly: the Paedagogus is not really a Messenger, he is playing at being a Messenger. We must not criticize him and the Messenger in the Antigone on the same principles. He is not charming: he has something else to do than to charm, and it is precisely because he is not charming that he is not undramatic. Look at the sweep of the speech. A quiet beginning leads to . . . a second and a greater climax . . . as the two remaining charioteers go round and round the course until the terrible end comes. . . . It is a magnificent piece of bravura [boldness], as we listen to it, watching the grimness behind it, observing its effect on the two women, who, fresh from their quarrel, hang upon every word. . . .

GREAT TECHNICAL MASTERY

This is a convenient point at which to consider what is in some ways Sophocles' masterpiece in the use of the three actors: the *Philoctetes*. It is very much of an actor's play; the subject offers little scope for lyricism [poetic expression], and the poet will not manufacture it. Ostensibly the subject is the plot laid by Odysseus against Philoctetes, and its failure; the dramatic interest is to watch how the young hero comes to realize, with increasing shame, how false and intolerable is the enterprise into which Odysseus has entrapped him; the theme that underlies the whole is that the Greek commanders at Troy are suffering the natural recoil [realization of the shame] of their past inhumanity to

Philoctetes. The action of the play moves forward, step by step, with a subtlety and a certainty not unworthy of comparison with the action of the *Tyrannus*. The three chief characters are brilliantly contrasted: the embittered and immovable Philoctetes, Odysseus the plausible villain, and the young Neoptolemus whose gradual transit from the side of Odysseus to that of Philoctetes is so absorbing a spectacle. The plot moves with the utmost freedom—yet, one is surprised to note, the *dramatis personae* [characters] in this quite unlyrical play are fewer than in any of the other six. They are in all only five. . . . To contrive so fluid a plot under such a severe restriction evinces great technical virtuosity.

Sophocles' Many Uses of the Chorus

G.M. Kirkwood

Of all the theatrical devices used by the ancient Greek dramatists, the chorus perhaps seems the strangest to modern audiences. Standing onstage during the entire play, the chorus periodically breaks into poetic songs, variously known as odes, *stasima* (singular, *stasimon*), and *parodoi* (singular, *parodos*). Often, the Greek chorus is too easily explained away simply as a group of observers who "comment" on the action of the story. The chorus does comment, of course, but it also can and does perform a multitude of other functions, depending on the situation and the inventiveness of the playwright. As former Cornell University professor G.M. Kirkwood shows in this excerpt from his book *A Study of Sophoclean Drama*, Sophocles was highly inventive in his employment of the chorus. Sometimes, the Sophoclean chorus sings odes that stand on their own and seem to bear little relation to the plot; at other times the chorus's poetic interludes actually move the plot along. Also, says Kirkwood, the chorus can itself become an independent character; take a character's side and staunchly defend his or her actions; or, as a diversion, provide the audience with needed, although temporary, relief from the emotional tensions created by a gripping story.

What part does the chorus play in Sophoclean drama? Most conspicuously, it sings lyrical songs. Many of the songs are of remarkable poetic grace, and some express deeply felt religious and moral ideas with great power and beauty. The lyrics of tragedy are, along with [the ancient Greek poet] Pindar, our main possession of Greek choral poetry.

Some of these songs can be read satisfactorily when detached from their context. The famous ode on man which is the first stasimon [choral song] of *Antigone*, the second stasimon of *Oedipus Tyrannus* with its prayer that the singers may live in piety under the law of heaven, the ode in praise of Colonus and Attica in *Oedipus at Colonus*, and the song in *Antigone* on Danae, Lycurgus, and Cleopatra are self-sufficient lyric poems, complete and enjoyable in themselves. If they had been transmitted to us alone, we could barely determine that they belonged in plays, and we could not possibly say from what kind of dramatic context they had been lifted. Other odes, while more extensively linked to the context [of plays], are still independent enough in content to be thoroughly intelligible alone: in *Ajax* the ode addressed to Salamis and that on the sorrows of war, Stasimon Two of *Antigone* on the troubles of the house of Labdacus, and the ode on old age in *OC* [*Oedipus at Colonus*]. Even in odes that are so closely woven into their context that they form a commentary on the immediate action, Sophocles has a way of starting with a general idea or a thought removed from the immediate matter and only later circling back to the situation of the play. . . .

The detachment that marks so many of Sophocles' choral songs raises problems when we think about the meaning of the odes in relation to the plays. If all the lyrics were as immediately and obviously concerned with the action as, for example, Stasimon Three of *The Trachinian Women*, in which the chorus reveal their recognition of what the oracle given to Heracles really meant and describe what Heracles has suffered and Deianeira done, we should have no serious trouble in assigning the lyrics their place in the action. Such an ode obviously has the simple function of providing a lyrical commentary on the events of the play. By the poetic intensity and grace of its diction and rhythm it adds a further dimension of meaning and dramatic force to those events. But immediacy and simplicity of reference are found in less than half the odes. There are also general reflections on the nature of man, on piety, on old age, on the beauties of Attica, on the power of love. What are we to make of these?

One way to dispose of [explain] them is to treat them simply as independent lyrics expressing Sophocles' thoughts about the various matters on which they touch. If they seem totally irrelevant, then never mind the context; their own beauty and profundity are enough to justify their presence, and convention demanded that the action of the play be broken by lyrical passages. This somewhat cavalier [casual] procedure is followed by some critics and probably many readers; we often see choral passages quoted, without context or reference to context, as examples of what Sophocles thought. . . .

THE CHORUS AS ONE OF THE ACTORS

There is another way of approach to the choral odes, an approach by which they are neither studied in a vacuum nor assumed to be Sophocles' sentiments. It is possible to assume that the odes spring from the mind of the chorus, as a character or, to be more exact, a group of undifferentiated characters of the drama in a precise set of circumstances, and to see what connection they have with the action that forms their context. The context need not be only the episodes immediately preceding and following. It may involve the structure and rhythm of the play as a whole, the personality of the chorus, their relation to the other persons of the drama. . . .

There are good reasons for using this approach. In the first place, there are some odes that quite obviously do not represent what Sophocles thought about the situation in hand but only what the group of persons forming the chorus thought, without suggesting either profundity [great insight] or vacuity [ignorance] in their thought. In Stasimon Two of *Ajax* the chorus joyfully and mistakenly think that Ajax will not commit suicide. The fact that the chorus are mistaken in their joy does not destroy the force of the song (in fact it helps to create its dramatic force), because it is not a mistaken moral judgment . . . but a mistaken view of events. Secondly, Sophoclean choral odes are quite conspicuously suited to the group of singers. Just those choral songs that seem most detached in content are sung by choruses that are most detached, grave, and self-reliant. The choral ode on old age is sung by old men; the ode in praise of Attica by Atticans. Nowhere in Sophocles' plays is there a contradiction in the attitude of the chorus between its songs and its other utterances. This adaptation of the content of choral songs to the attitude and personality of the singers does not arise by accident.

We have external evidence both from a highly reputable critic who undoubtedly knew more of Sophocles' plays than we do and from Sophocles himself that suggests that this approach is valid: in praising the Sophoclean chorus Aristotle clearly implies that it has its place in the drama as "one of the actors.". . . There is [also] Sophocles' capacity for remaining inside the myth and never stepping outside it to explain or to reveal to us his point of view about what is happening. If we look for the sentiments of the poet in Sophoclean odes, we are in search of what is unlikely to be presented explicitly by a playwright whose whole way of procedure is not to criticize and reshape but to work within the myth. . . .

There are two distinct types of personal relationship between the choral group and the action and persons around them. The choruses of *Ajax*, *The Trachinian Women*, *Electra*, and *Philoctetes* are closely attached each to one character: to Ajax, Deianeira, Electra, and Neoptolemus, respectively. In these four plays the choruses are by no means impartial; their sympathies . . . are with a single person, and they share his point of view. They do not echo every word of their champion, for they are not merely extensions of his personality; they have their own nature and some independence of thought. The sailors in *Ajax* warn their leader against undue boastfulness, and those in *Philoctetes* express their sympathy for Philoctetes before Neoptolemus has begun to feel any. But in the larger issues they stand firm with their favorite's prejudices and interests as they see them: Ajax's men are as mistakenly bitter toward Odysseus as Ajax is. . . .

In the other three plays the choruses are more independent. In *Antigone* and *Oedipus at Colonus* it is clear that, wherever their sympathies may lie, the choruses are primarily elders of Thebes and Colonus, respectively, and their attitude to what is going on is always shaped by the responsibilities and special interests of their position. In *Oedipus Tyrannus* they are devoted to Oedipus; but in the very passage in which they most firmly state their devotion, it is quite clear that they feel a civic rather than a strictly personal loyalty (unlike the chorus of *Ajax*); it is Oedipus as savior of Thebes whom they revere: "For the winged maiden came upon him, a manifest thing, and in the test he was proved wise and a blessing to the city; therefore he shall never be judged guilty of evil by my judgment.". . .

DEPENDENT AND INDEPENDENT CHORUSES

We are now ready to look at the choral songs, the parodoi and stasima, sung by the chorus alone. We shall find that the

distinction between two choral relationships to the drama
. . . is only a preliminary issue here and will only help a little
toward clarifying this part of the chorus's role. Even in choral
odes where we can clearly detect an air of independent judgment there is much more to be taken into account. But a beginning can be made with this point. We have noticed that
those odes that have, beyond others, an air of detachment are
sung by choruses whose measure of independence as persons is greatest: Stasimon One of *Antigone*, Stasimon Two of
Oedipus Tyrannus, Stasimon One of *Oedipus at Colonus*. Is
there a corresponding immediacy and dependence in odes
sung by choruses who are personally dependent? . . .

In *Ajax*, from the opening words "Telamonian Ajax,"
throughout the song, the chorus express their concern, devotion, and dependence. In *The Trachinian Women* the bur-
den of the parodos is Heracles: Where is he? May he come!
Zeus will protect him. But the chorus are thinking about
Heracles from Deianeira's point of view; they are grieved by
her grief and concern for him, and they urge her to be confident. There is not, certainly, dependence as in *Ajax*, but
there is intense personal sympathy. In *Antigone* and *Oedipus
Tyrannus* there is concern also, but concern for the city of
Thebes. In *Antigone* the theme of the ode is joy and pride at
the victory of Thebes over the Seven, with a counterpoint of
sorrow for the death of the two sons of Oedipus. In *OT* [*Oedipus Tyrannus*] the ode is a cry of distress at the plight of
Thebes and a prayer to the gods to help Thebes against the
ravages of plague.

Once again, then, we find the familiar distinction between
personal and impersonal, attached and independent choruses. To pursue our analysis throughout the odes would be
tedious and unnecessary; we should find that the same relation between the personality of the choral group and the nature of its songs is steadily maintained. . . .

HOW SOPHOCLES' CHORUSES DIFFERED
FROM THOSE OF HIS RIVALS

To see that this careful and consistent relating of choral
songs to choral personality is distinctively Sophoclean, it
will be useful to look for a moment at some aspects of the
choral manner of Aeschylus and Euripides. The choruses of
Aeschylus are certainly dramatic, though not all of them in
the same way. One type is most strikingly exemplified by *The*

Suppliants, where the choral group is, of course, the protagonist. . . . A different kind of dramatic chorus appears in *The
Persians* and, with more imposing grandeur, in *Agamemnon*; here the episodes are, broadly speaking, illustrations of
the theme, which finds its fullest expression and is made
universal in the choral odes. Euripides sometimes uses the
chorus in this second Aeschylean manner. In *The Trojan
Women* . . . the lyrics are the shaping and unifying element of
the play. . . .

It never has been suggested, so far as I know, that any
chorus of Sophocles is the protagonist; but it has often been
supposed that his choruses convey the dramatic theme,
more or less in the manner of *Agamemnon*. . . .

Euripides clearly did not have the same interest as Sophocles in preserving the "character" of the chorus in the sense
of carefully adapting the thought and manner of the songs to
the personality and situation of the choral group. Nor is this
difference just a matter of choral personality; it tells us
something about the difference in attitude between Sophocles and Euripides toward dramatic structure. In the choral
odes as elsewhere Euripides is the more detached and abstract playwright; with Sophocles everything is personal and
immediate. It does not at all follow that Euripidean dramatic
form is inferior, only that it is different and that it does not
have the same kind of unbroken tension that is the hallmark
of Sophoclean form.

USING THE CHORUS TO MOVE THE PLOT ALONG

In this comparison of Sophoclean and Euripidean manner
we are . . . dealing with a question of structure as well as
choral personality. We must now, in order to complete our
account of Sophocles' disposal of his chorus, look at several
further aspects of it that bear more essentially on structure
than on character drawing. . . .

In the parodos of *Antigone* the chorus tell of the defeat of
the Argive army and the triumph of Thebes. Immediately
after it Creon enters and makes his specious inaugural address. In *Antigone* . . . the prologue and the first episode introduce two different elements of the theme. The parodos is
accommodated to this structure; the Theban elders know
nothing of Antigone's anger or her determination to flout the
edict of the new monarch, and their song of victory is in
complete contrast to the passion and excitement of the pro-

logue. Its connection with the following scene is just the reverse of this relationship of contrast. With its dominant
theme of victory it provides exactly the right tone for the introduction of the scene. It also, of course, gives information
about the repulse of the invading army, but what is dramatically important is its spirit, which blends perfectly with the
proud and confident tone of Creon's opening address and
thus contributes to the ultimate irony of the contrast between this lofty beginning and the tumultuous and undigni-
fied incident after the guard's arrival. Thus the tone of the
ode, by its contrast with what goes before and its adaptation
to the mood that follows, is structurally valuable.

The parodos of *Oedipus Tyrannus* adapts the same principle to different circumstances. In the prologue Creon returns
from Delphi to announce that the plague will end only if the
murderer of Laius is driven from Thebes. The first episode
begins with Oedipus' proclamation to the people, commanding them to reveal the murderer if they can. There is no contrast, in the spirit or content, between the two scenes; *Oedipus* is a play of continuous dramatic development. There
might therefore seem to be no dramatic use for the parodos
beyond linking prologue to episode by lyrical repetition of
key ideas in the prologue. . . . Certainly the parodos does perform this service, but it also does more, and its additional
role is typically Sophoclean. The song has three themes: inquiry about the meaning of the oracle, lament for the ravages
of the plague, and prayer invoking the aid of Athena,
Artemis, Apollo, Zeus, and Dionysus. All three are continua-
tions of themes begun in the prologue, but that of prayer,
which is dominant in the ode, has an additional force. . . .

A Song to Relieve the Tension

There is one more kind of structural effect achieved by
Sophoclean choral odes that deserves mention, although it is
essentially a negative effect: while the odes we have been
noticing have, by contrast or suspense or ambiguity, created
or enhanced dramatic tension, these odes to some degree
relax the intensity of a situation. Perhaps they are no more
than instances of songs in the "classical style," but two of
them in particular, *Oedipus Tyrannus* and *Antigone*, have so
pronounced an effect on the rhythm of the dramatic action
that they require separate mention.

The *Oedipus* ode begins with an agonized lament for the

fate of mankind:

> Woe for the generations of man! Your lives are equal to noth-
> ingness in my reckoning. What man ever has more of pros-
> perity than its mere seeming, and after the seeming, a decline?

Then, in a lyrical review of Oedipus' greatness and suffering, the chorus give voice to the emotional stress that has
been built up almost beyond endurance in the terrible incident that precedes, and by giving voice to it they bring a
measure of relief. Gloomy and despairing though their cry
is, it yet calms and brings a lull in the action. . . . Structurally
the function of the ode is modest, but its fine emotional con-
summation of the catastrophe makes it at once lyrically
great and dramatically appropriate.

In *Antigone* the corresponding ode is sung just after
Antigone has been led off to be imprisoned. It tells of three
imprisonments: of Danae, Lycurgus, and Cleopatra. It is a
striking poem. . . . Here, as generally, the contribution of the
ode is very simple: instead of moral pronouncement we have
a poetic elaboration, very moving and vivid, of the single
theme of imprisonment, forming a kind of lyrical finale to
the foregoing scene. It is the emotion of the chorus, and the
imaginative reach of their song, not their intellectual
prowess, that count here. . . . The ode is a transformation of
the pathos of events into lyrical terms that fulfill and give
respite from the tragic action. Then the plot is renewed with
the Teiresias scene.

USING THE CHORUS TO PREACH?

Finally, something should be said about the second stasimon
of *Oedipus Tyrannus.* Of its two lyrical systems, the first contains a prayer for piety and reverence and a condemnation of
hybris [arrogance]; the second expresses the hope that evil
practices may be punished and ends with the fervent wish
that Apollo's oracles may be fulfilled and the fear that religion is vanishing from the earth. Because of its devoutly religious tone the ode creates a very strong impression. It is
frequently made to bear an interpretative weight in relation
to the play as a whole that it does not deserve. To one critic
this is one of just two passages "where we feel certain that
Sophocles is preaching." But if Sophocles is preaching here,
what is the point of the sermon in relation to the play? Does
it charge Oedipus with *hybris*? . . . It is extremely difficult to
find confirmation in the rest of the play for this judgment,

and therefore we may well hesitate to regard it as such. . . .

What, then, are the dramatic qualities of the ode? First, it is relevant to the context—not just because it discusses topics that have a place in the episodes before and after, but also, and mainly, because the manner in which the chorus make their reflections is fitting both to the personality of the elders and to the dramatic atmosphere in which the ode is set. Secondly, instead of interrupting the course of the drama with a sermon by Sophocles, settling moral and religious problems, the words of this ode simply express, in language of vigor and beauty, the religious thoughts of the chorus, evoked by their doubts and anxiety. The ode settles nothing. But as in the *Antigone* odes the very ambiguity and inconclusiveness of the song increase dramatic tension, where a sermon would break it. Finally, there is a distinctively Sophoclean touch in the ironical interplay between the ode, Jocasta's prayer, and the appearance of the Corinthian.

The above sketch of how the chorus fits into Sophoclean drama is frankly incomplete. An attempt to give an exhaustive account would necessitate discussion of imagery and meter and study of the thought of the odes at some length. . . . We have seen that, consistently and effectively, Sophocles keeps the spirit and the thought of his choral songs in line with the personality and the immediate position and attitude of the group of singers. And we have seen also that he often goes beyond this kind of dramatic relevance to create various effects of contrast, suspense, relief, irony, and ambiguity, which contribute to the effectiveness of the action. . . . The choral group is a character, and its personality and its relation to other characters are worked out with the same skill that Sophocles expends on the rest of his character portrayal; and the choral songs are integral parts of the dramatic structure, contributing, like the other parts, to the compact shape and the subtle rhythm of the whole.

Sophocles' Comic Relief: The Satyr Plays

William Nickerson Bates

All of the great ancient Greek playwrights wrote satyr
plays, usually short, rollicking, and often obscene
farces. These less serious plays were presented at the
City Dionysia dramatic festivals as a kind of comic
relief to keep audiences from being totally over-
whelmed by the horror and gloom of the more stately
tragedies. Like all Greek drama, the satyr plays originated in the religious rituals of the dim past, particularly in the celebrations known as dithyrambs. These
were held to honor the god Dionysus, son of Zeus,
leader of the gods. The Greeks pictured Dionysus as
half-man and half-goat and associated him with fertility, wine, the cycle of the seasons, and the recurring natural pattern of birth, maturity, death, and
rebirth. The dithyramb ceremonies consisted mainly
of prayer and sacrifice followed by colorful processions. Wearing costumes and masks often representing goats, the worshipers, also known as revelers,
"mummed," or acted out in pantomime, traditional
stories about Dionysus and other gods. In the
following essay, William Nickerson Bates, a former
professor of Greek literature at the University of
Pennsylvania, discusses the development of satyr
plays and how those Sophocles wrote were little
known until the early years of the twentieth century.

No adequate knowledge of the satyr drama of Sophocles was
available to modern scholars previous to the publication in
1912 of a papyrus containing considerable portions of the
Ichneutae, or *Trackers.* Before that time the great dramatist
had regularly been thought of as supreme among the tragic
poets of Greece, and little if any attention was paid to the

From William Nickerson Bates, *Sophocles: Poet and Dramatist* (New York: Russell &
Russell, 1940). Reprinted by permission of the University of Pennsylvania Press.

scanty fragments of the satyr dramas which he was known to have written. This is not surprising when one remembers the meagerness of those fragments and, furthermore, that there is no statement in ancient literature that his satyr plays enjoyed any particular fame. In fact, in contrast with what we are told about the satyr dramas of Aeschylus the natural inference would be that they did not. Thus the general opinion of scholars before the publication of the papyrus seems to have been that such satyr plays as Sophocles wrote were composed in order to conform to a convention of the Attic stage with no special excellence of their own. That he could have entered into this form of composition with spirit and with evident enjoyment could not have been anticipated.

SONG OF THE GOAT MEN

In its origin the satyr drama goes very far back in the history of the Greek people. According to Suidas [or Suda Lexicon, a tenth-century Greek encyclopedia], Arion from Methymna in Lesbos, who lived at the court of Periander of Corinth [an important ancient city-state], first set up a chorus and sang the dithyramb; that he gave the name to the song sung by the chorus, and introduced satyrs speaking in verse. This would take us back to the latter part of the seventh century B.C. but we cannot imagine satyrs appearing then for the first time. Mumming has always been a favorite amusement among primitive peoples, especially in connection with religious rites, and we cannot be far wrong if we imagine that men dressed themselves in goat skins with horses' tails and took part in religious dances and songs at a very early period.

It has been generally recognized that from some such form of the dithyramb as that presented by Arion tragedy was derived; that men dressed in goat skins played the part of satyrs, the traditional companions of Dionysus, in whose honor the performance was being held; and that tragedy got its name from the song of these goat men. But the satyrs soon dropped out as an essential element in the performance, and tragedy was left to develop along its own lines without them. This was the case also with comedy. We cannot, however, imagine the satyr choruses as being altogether discontinued. They were too deeply rooted in the affections of the people ever to have been completely abandoned. It is, indeed, probable that they were kept up in an impromptu way during the time that tragedy and comedy were attaining definite form until, like them, the satyr drama was evolved as a distinct dramatic type.

The first man to write satyr dramas, according to Suidas, was Pratinas, an older contemporary of Aeschylus. This statement probably means that he was the first to give them literary form. He specialized in this type of composition, as is clear from the statement that of the fifty plays which he is said to have written thirty-two were satyr dramas. They enjoyed a great reputation in antiquity [ancient times]. Pausanias [a noted Greek traveler and writer], writing in the second century A.D., says that after those of Aeschylus the satyr plays of Pratinas and of his son Aristias were the most famous.

Like tragedy, the satyr drama no doubt underwent a development which cannot now be traced. In modern times previous to the publication of the *Ichneutae* papyrus it was known from the *Cyclops* of Euripides, the only example of this type of composition to come down in the regular channels of literary tradition. From that play we learn that the satyr drama was short. The *Cyclops* has 709 lines, or about half the length of the average tragedy; but in form it is more like tragedy than comedy. The episodes and the lyric parts are short and there are no formal stasima [songs sung by the chorus]; and, furthermore, the lyric metres are simple, implying that the dances were simple as would be expected. . . . There is also a certain amount of coarseness which would have been entirely out of place in tragedy.

During the great period of the Attic stage we find a satyr play regularly forming the fourth member of the tetralogy [group of four plays] with which the tragic poets competed against one another. Who first adopted this arrangement there is no means of knowing. Perhaps it was Aeschylus, to whom the Athenians were indebted for so many innovations in their theatre. He used the satyr drama in that way, whereas Pratinas evidently did not, as the number of his plays shows. But the custom was beginning to give way as early as 438 B.C., when Euripides concluded a tetralogy with the *Alcestis*. It is known, however, that satyr dramas continued to be performed down into late Greek times.

THE KNOWN SATYR PLAYS

When we come to consider the works of the three great tragic poets we find that eight titles of Aeschylus are definitely known to have been those of satyr plays. They are the

Cercyon, the *Circe,* the *Kerykes,* the *Leon,* the *Lycurgus,* the *Prometheus,* the *Proteus,* and the *Sphinx*; and about as many more may with some reason be added to this list.

In the case of Euripides . . . seven titles are known. They are the *Autolycus,* the *Busiris,* the *Cyclops,* the *Eurystheus,* the *Sciron,* the *Syleus,* and the *Theristae.*

SILENUS SCOLDS THE SATYRS

In this excerpt from the surviving fragments of Sophocles' Ichneutae, *Silenus and a chorus made up of his fellow satyrs have agreed to help the god Apollo look for a lost herd of cattle. While searching, they hear a strange sound issuing from a dark cave, and when the satyrs express their fear of the noise Silenus scolds them.*

CHORUS

Just listen to the thing a little while–
A sound such as no mortal ever heard
By which we have been startled and aroused.

SILENUS

Why fear a noise? Why are ye [you] so alarmed
With your accursed bodies made of wax,
Ye worst of beasts who see a frightful sight
In every shadow, scared at everything?
It's feeble service, slovenly and base
That ye perform, and if one looks at ye
He finds ye tongue and phallus [penis], nothing else. . . .
I never turned to flight, no coward I;
I did not crouch in terror at the noise
Of mountain-nurtured beasts, but with my spear
Did glorious deeds perform which now by ye
Are tarnished by some humbug shepherd's noise. . . .
Unless ye find the path and track those cows
To see where with their herder they have gone,
Your cowardice itself will be the cause
Of weeping on your part and noise, too.

For Sophocles we have a longer list. Seventeen of his plays may be identified as satyr dramas either because they are expressly designated as such by some ancient writer, or because the extant [surviving] fragments make it clear that they could not have been tragedies. These are the *Amphiaraus,* the *Amycus,* the *Cedalion,* the *Dionysiscus,* the *Heracleïscus,* the *Heracles at Taenarum,* the *Hybris,* the *Ichneutae,* the *Inachus*, the *Kophoi*, the *Krisis*, the *Lovers of Achilles*, the *Marriage of Helen*, the *Momus*, the *Pandora*, the *Salmoneus*, and the *Telephus*. Besides these there are eight other titles which may with varying degrees of probability be regarded as belonging to satyr dramas. With the exception of the *Ichneutae* the fragments of all these plays are so short that at first sight they might seem to afford little evidence for reconstructing their plots. Since the publication of the papyrus, however, many of them have taken on new significance, for knowing how Sophocles handled his material we are now in a position to recover something of the plots of most of them. . . . We learn from the *Ichneutae* that Sophocles did not hesitate to alter a traditional story in order to bring about a dramatic situation; and, furthermore, that in his satyr dramas Dionysus might have little or nothing to do with the plot. An ancient tale might thus easily be converted into a rollicking farce which might come as a welcome relief to an audience which had just been listening to three tragedies.

When one looks over what is left of these satyr plays he cannot help being surprised that the great tragic poet who produced such masterpieces as the *Oedipus Tyrannus*, the *Antigone*, and the *Electra* could stoop to such compositions. But Sophocles had a sense of humor and could indulge in fun where it was appropriate, as in these satyr dramas. A study of their fragments reveals the dramatist in a very different light; and the finding of a large part of one of them, which had been copied at the end of the second century A.D. with marginal notes on the text, astonishing as it may seem, proves that, like the tragedies, they were studied by scholars and like them were read and enjoyed down into late Greek times.

CHAPTER 2

Oedipus the King

READINGS ON
SOPHOCLES

The Oedipus Legend

Bernard M.W. Knox

The following selection is a portion of the introduction to a well-known 1959 translation of Sophocles'
Oedipus the King by the noted classical scholar and
former associate professor at Yale University,
Bernard M.W. Knox. In his usual clear and concise
style, Knox first explains how the ancient Greek
dramatists took most of their stories directly from
popular myths, which meant that the audience knew
the plots in advance. Then he provides a brief
overview of the first section of the Oedipus myth,
consisting of the main characters and events that
directly precede the opening of the play itself.

Sophocles and his fellow dramatists used for their plays stories of a time long past which were the familiar heritage of
all Athenians—stories they had learned from their parents
and would pass on to their children in their turn. To a large
extent, then, the element of novelty, which is characteristic of
the modern theater, was missing, though the stories were so
rich in variants and so flexible in detail that minor surprises
were possible and were often provided. But what the dramatist lost in novelty he gained in other ways. The myths he
used gave to his plays, without any effort on his part, some of
those larger dimensions of authority which the modern
dramatist must create out of nothing if his play is to be more
than a passing entertainment. The myths had the authority of
history, for myth is in one of its aspects the *only* history of an
age that kept no records. They had also the authority inherent in moral and religious symbols, for the myths served as
typical patterns of the conduct of man and the manifestation
of the gods. They were stories in which the historical, moral
and religious experience of the whole race was distilled.

The myths gave the ancient dramatist another advantage.
One of the most difficult problems facing the modern drama-

tist—exposition, the indication early in the play of the background of his characters and their situation—was, for the ancient dramatist, no problem at all. He had only to indicate the identity of the characters and the point in the story where his play began, and the job was done. He could limit his exposition to emphasizing those particular details of the background which were important for his own treatment of the story.

THEBES IN CRISIS

A priest describes the nature of Thebes's recent troubles to the king, Oedipus, in this excerpt from the opening scene of the play, Oedipus the King.

PRIEST

Oedipus, ruler of Thebes, you see us here at your altar,
men of all ages—some not yet strong enough to fly far from
the nest, others heavy with age, priests, of Zeus in my case,
and these are picked men from the city's youth. The rest of
the Thebans, carrying boughs like us, are sitting in the mar-
ket place, at the two temples of Athena, and at the prophetic
fire of Apollo near the river Ismenus.

You can see for yourself—the city is like a ship rolling
dangerously; it has lost the power to right itself and raise its
head up out of the waves of death. Thebes is dying. There is
a blight on the crops of the land, on the ranging herds of
cattle, on the stillborn labor of our women. The fever-god
swoops down on us, hateful plague, he hounds the city and
empties the houses of Thebes. The black god of death is
made rich with wailing and funeral laments.

The audience, once it recognized the story, knew what had preceded the action of the play. But it knew even more. It knew more or less accurately what was going to happen in the play itself. And this fact enabled the ancient dramatist to work in a vein which is characteristic of Greek tragedy and especially of Sophocles—dramatic irony. Everything said by the characters in the play means more to the audience than it does to the speaker. For the audience knows more than he does, knows the truth about the past (which Oedipus, for example, does not know) and the truth about the future. The audience during the play is in fact in the position of the gods, and is able to see the struggles, hopes and fears of the characters against a background of the truth—past, present and future. This situation gives to the dramatic action as a whole an intensity and complication which is the hallmark of Greek tragedy; the audience understands everything on two different levels at once. It is involved emotionally in the blind heroic efforts of Oedipus, a man like each of them; and it is detached from those efforts by its superior knowledge, the knowledge of the gods. Ancient tragedy gives the spectator an image of his own life, not only as he sees it and lives it himself, but as it must look to the all-seeing eye of divine knowledge.

This somber irony shows itself not only in the larger frame of the action but in details, too. One speech after another in the play uses the audience's knowledge to provide a dramatic shock. Jocasta's speech to Oedipus on her first entrance, with its scolding, nagging tone that suggests a mother reproving a wayward son; the answer of the chorus to the Corinthian messenger, "This lady is ... his wife and mother of his children"; Oedipus' statement that he will fight on behalf of Laius "as if he were my own father"—all these dramatic hammer blows are made possible by the fact that the audience knows the story to begin with.

RESCUED FROM DEATH

The story is old, strange and terrible. Laius and Jocasta, the childless king and queen of Thebes, were told by the god Apollo that their son would kill his father and marry his mother. A son was born to them, and they tried to make sure that the prophecy would not come true. Laius drove a metal pin through the infant's ankles and gave it to a shepherd, with instructions to leave it to die of exposure on the nearby mountain, Cithaeron. The shepherd took the child up to the mountain, but pitied it and gave it to a fellow shepherd he met there, who came from Corinth, on the other side of the mountain range. This shepherd took the child with him and gave it to the childless king and queen of Corinth, Polybus and Merope. They brought the child up as their own son, and named him Oedipus, which in its Greek form *Oidipous* means "swollen foot" (his feet had been injured by the metal pin). So Oedipus grew up in Corinth as the king's son, with no idea of his real parentage. And Laius and Jocasta believed that their child was dead and the prophecy of Apollo false.

After Oedipus became a young man, he was told, by a man who had drunk too much at a banquet, that he was not the real son of Polybus. He was reassured by Polybus and

Merope, but a lingering doubt remained and rumors were spreading abroad. He went, on his own initiative, to Delphi, in the north of Greece, to the oracle of Apollo, to ask the god who his parents were. All he was told was that he would kill his father and marry his mother. He resolved never to return to Corinth, to Polybus and Merope, and started out to make a new life for himself elsewhere. He came to a place where three main roads met, and in the narrow place was ordered off the road and then attacked by the driver of a chariot in which an old man was riding. A fight started, and Oedipus, in self-defense, killed the old man and his attendants—all except one, who escaped and took the news to Thebes. The old man in the chariot was Laius, king of Thebes. And so the first half of the prophecy of Apollo was fulfilled. Oedipus, though he did not know it, had killed his father.

THE PROPHECY FULFILLED

Oedipus continued on his way, and came to Thebes. He found the city in distress. A monster, the Sphinx—part bird, part lion, part woman—was killing the young men of Thebes and refused to go away until someone answered her riddle. Many had tried, but all had failed, and met their death. The Thebans offered a great reward to anyone who could answer the riddle of the Sphinx—the throne of Thebes and the hand of Jocasta, the widowed queen, in marriage. Oedipus volunteered to answer the riddle: "There is a creature two-footed, and also four-footed, and three-footed. It has one voice. When it goes on most feet, then it goes most slowly." Oedipus answered the riddle correctly. The answer is Man, who goes on all fours as a child, on two feet as an adult and on three as an old man, since he has a stick to help him along.

Oedipus married Jocasta and became king of Thebes. The prophecy was fulfilled, but he did not realize it. For many years he ruled Thebes well, an admired and just king. He had two daughters and two sons. And then a plague broke out in Thebes. The people of the city died, the cattle died, the crops rotted. The Thebans thronged the temples and a delegation of priests went to the palace to beg Oedipus to save them. These are the priests who come on stage at the beginning of the play, and as they enter, the stage door opens and a masked actor comes out and addresses them. The play has begun.

An Overview of *Oedipus the King*

Sheldon Cheney

The pitiful characters and horrifying plot twists of Sophocles' *Oedipus the King* emerged from the mists of ancient legend perhaps more than three thousand years ago. They remain morbidly fascinating, compelling, and capable of stirring as much revulsion in modern audiences as they did in ancient ones. For those as yet unfamiliar with Oedipus's classic tale of woe, noted theater historian Sheldon Cheney penned the following synopsis. What makes this overview of the play stand out from most others is that Cheney describes the characters and action, and even some of the crucial lines, as they would have appeared during an actual performance in an ancient Greek theater.

A herald! Yes, now he is calling forth Sophocles, first of this year's contestants for the tragedy prize. And the play is on. For there, around the altar of the dancing-circle, a crowd of "supers" has gathered, Theban citizens, miserable, suppliant. And one stands a little apart, a priest. Forth to them comes an actor, majestically, masked and in kingly robes. His voice breaks into the morning silence with startling resonance, with the measured stately beauty of words severely chosen, richly intoned.

> My children, fruit of Cadmus' ancient tree
> New springing, wherefore thus with bended knee
> Press ye upon us, laden all with wreaths
> And suppliant branches? And the city breathes
> Heavy with incense, heavy with dim prayer
> And shrieks to affright the Slayer.
>   . . . Seeing 'tis I ye call,
> 'Tis I am come, world-honored Oedipus.

Ah, this then will be the story of Oedipus the King, most tragic, most terrible. This actor and the priest now are telling

From Sheldon Cheney, *Three Thousand Years of Drama, Acting, and Stagecraft* (London: Longmans, Greene, 1929).

ϽΒdy know (our minds flash back to the old
dipus, having slain the Sphinx and delivered
the widowed Queen Jocasta, ruled happily
ι found a pestilence destroying his city. We
_ᴜ, ιoo horrible almost for words: that this pesti-
.ϲιιce has come from the gods, because all unwittingly Oedipus has killed his own father, the former king, and now is
married to his own mother. But these characters in the play,
this proud Oedipus, and the Queen whom Sophocles will
make so noble, so touching, they do not know. Like the gods
themselves, this day we shall watch the fearful truth unfold
to these two.

THE FIRST CLIMAX

Oedipus and the Priest have told us now the misery of the
Theban people; and the King—oh, irony!—pledges to seek
out the cause of the sorrow, to cast it out at whatever cost.
But now the Suppliants crowd toward the gateway beyond
the orchestra, where Creon is entering. He, the brother of Jocasta, comes from Delphi with messages from the Oracle:
there is an unclean one in the land, he who slew Laius, the
former king, and he is to be punished before the blight can
be lifted. We watch as Oedipus and Creon build in dialogue
toward the first climax: to that moment when the King goes
back through the palace door—yes, that simple proscenium
[stage archway] has become to us a palace now—vowing to
search out the slayer of Laïus.

The Suppliants give way to the Chorus of Theban Elders.
Half-chanting they come, half-dancing, with slow stateli-
ness, threading their way over the dance-circle, taking up
position as prayers to Apollo:
"A voice, a voice, that is borne on the Holy Way.". . . Here
indeed is the old religious dancing-procession, here the old
devotional pattern showing through the design of the new
human drama. They chant, they repeat the story of the pestilence, they implore the mercy of the gods, they call on
Apollo, Athena, Artemis, Zeus, Dionysus.

Oedipus is coming again forward from the palace. He
speaks, he ponders, he calls on the guilty slayer of Laïus to
come forth and be banished. He sends for the blind prophet
Tiresius. We listen to these two, the King ruthlessly tracking
down clue after clue, the old prophet holding back the
knowledge—till spurred beyond control:

> Thou art thyself the unclean thing!

We see the deluge of Oedipus' wrath at this incredible accusation, until the patient Tiresius pours forth his whole prophecy, foreshadows the tragedy to its end:

> Thou dost seek
> With threats and loud proclaim the man whose hand
> Slew Laïus. Lo, I tell thee, he doth stand
> Here ...
> His staff groping before him, he shall crawl
> O'er unknown earth, and voices round him call:
> "Behold the brother-father of his own
> Children, the seed, the sower and the sown,
> Shame to his mother's blood, and to his sire
> Son, murderer, incest-worker."

Like a relief from storm the Chorus comes, bringing a lyrical interlude, chanting, commenting upon the ways of gods and men, affirming faith in Oedipus—and relieving the tension with the sheer visual beauty of the dance-design.

A NEW DREAD

But Creon returns, eager to defend himself against Oedipus' charge that he has instigated the accusation against the King; and as these two come near to an encounter with swords, Jocasta enters before us:

> Vain men, what would ye with this angry swell
> Of words heart-blinded? Is there in your eyes
> No pity, thus, when all our city lies
> Bleeding, to ply your privy hates? ...

And it is she who brings to her King the first gleam of self-doubt. We see him now, losing his assurance, a dread beginning to creep in. He tells how once he killed a noble in a chariot, where three roads crossed. He was fleeing from Corinth; a prophecy had said he would kill his father and marry his mother—and so he had fled the court. And meeting this old man on the way, he had killed him and his guards. But Jocasta, stirred now by a deeper dread, sends for a herdsman, since banished to the hills, who saw Laius murdered.

We of the audience settle back, and let the strain fall a little from us as Oedipus and Jocasta go in; we note the strophes and antistrophes [poetic verses] of the Chorus rather idly—we have come to a human suspense that lyrics and dance cannot beguile us from. Now here is Jocasta again before us saying,

> So dire a storm
> Doth shake the king, sin, dread and every form
> Of grief . . .

But, as she prays to Apollo, a Stranger arrives by the gateway, hailing the Chorus, asking for the King. For a moment we are inclined to find relief, with Jocasta, in the news he brings. The King of Corinth, Oedipus' reputed father, is dead, and the old prophecy of patricide seems disproved. But suddenly a new dread is aroused. The Stranger discloses that Oedipus was not Corinthian at all, but was a Theban babe rescued from a wild mountainside where he had been left to die.

Ah, mark you, while this unfolds between Oedipus and the Stranger, how Jocasta turns aside, a sickness growing in her mind! Will no one there notice her as she totters?—now her head goes down into her hands. She knows! This King, her husband, is her own babe. No need to wait the coming of the herdsman. A quick effort to restrain Oedipus from seeking confirmation; then she goes, in horror, hardly daring a farewell. For us in the audience *her* tragedy is already complete. The Chorus this time interrupts only for a moment. All eyes watch for the herdsman's coming.

MORE HORRIBLE HAPPENINGS

How crisply Oedipus questions him! On the brink of disastrous knowledge, he searches out the reluctant truth with uncanny directness, without mercy. This is an inevitable structure. We see circumstance after circumstance nailed in; till suddenly Oedipus shines out—we know it is like this in his own mind—with all the guilty knowledge on him: himself son of Laius, murderer of his own father, incestuous husband to his own mother, brother to his own children! As he rushes into the palace, this time, we have need of the letdown of the choral interlude. Still we have little heart for the lyrical comment—for we know that at this very moment, offstage, the physical climax of the play is taking place. We know that a Messenger, as is the wont [usual custom], will come and recount to us the more horrible happenings, which perchance we could never have faced in the actual acting-out, under this pitiless morning sunshine. Now the Messenger is before us speaking:

> Like one entranced with passion, through the gate
> She passed, the white hands flashing o'er her head,

Like blades that tear, and fled, unswerving fled,
Toward her old bridal room, and disappeared
And the doors crashed behind her. But we heard
Her voice within, crying to him of old,
Her Laïus, long dead . . .
And, after that, I know not how her death
Found her. For sudden, with a roar of wrath,
Burst Oedipus upon us. Then, I ween,
We marked no more what passion held the Queen . . .
He dashed him on the chamber door. The straight
Door-bar of oak, it bent beneath his weight,
Shook from its sockets free, and in he burst
To the dark chamber.
     There we saw her first
Hanged, swinging from a noose, like a dead bird.
He fell back when he saw her. Then we heard
A miserable groan, and straight he found
And loosed the strangling knot, and on the ground
Laid her.—Ah, then the sight of horror came!
The pin of gold, broad-beaten like a flame,
He tore from off her breast, and, left and right,
Down on the shuddering orbits of his sight
Dashed it: "Out! Out! Ye never more shall see
Me nor the anguish nor the sins of me . . ."
     . . . Like a song
His voice rose, and again, again, the strong
And stabbing hand fell, and the massacred
And bleeding eyeballs streamed upon his beard,
Wild rain, and gouts of hail amid the rain.
    . . . All that eye or ear
Hath ever dreamed of misery is here.

THE LAST OF SIGHTS, THE LAST OF DAYS

And then Oedipus is led in before us, blinded and bleeding.
The old men of the Chorus turn away to escape the sight. But
in a sort of sick horror we face this broken King, this abased
human being. He gropes his way forward, calling on the
gods, glorying that he has made himself a dungeon, "dark,
without sound . . . self-prisoned from a world of pain," curs-
ing the shepherd who saved him as a babe.

O flesh, horror of flesh! . . .
    In God's name,
Take me somewhere far off and cover me
From sight, or slay, or cast me to the sea
Where never eye may see me any more.

But now he has one thought more: his children, his two little daughters. There they are, Creon is bringing them before
us and him.

> Children! Where are ye? Hither; come to these
> Arms of your—brother, whose wild offices
> Have brought much darkness on the once bright eyes
> Of him who grew your garden; who, nowise
> Seeing nor understanding, digged a ground
> The world shall shudder at . . .
> > Creon, thou alone art left
> Their father now, since both of us are gone
> Who cared for them. Oh, leave them not alone.
> > . . . So young they are, so desolate—
> Of all save thee. True man, give me thine hand,
> And promise . . .

For a moment only he weakens, and clings to the children. But we see them dragged from him. Creon says, "Seek not to be master more." And as Oedipus is led away, the Chorus chants again. As it too disappears, we are warned:

> Therefore, O Man, beware, and look toward the end of
> > things that be,
> The last of sights, the last of days; and no man's life account
> > as gain
> Ere the full tale be finished and the darkness find him with-
> > out pain.

At the end of this utterly moving, purging, terrible drama, we spectators wake gradually to the world about us. There is something absurdly trivial about the things we do when the Chorus has finally disappeared: we stand and stretch, and perhaps turn a little away from the sun—and titter because a man is sobbing near us. Our feelings are very close to the surface, and we have a tendency to lose sight of the audience around us in recurring fits of "star-gazing." We are shaken—and yet there is a glow of beauty in our souls, a brooding, a healing ecstasy. We have been through high grief, have descended into terror and sorrow, so terrible that all the pettinesses of life have been stripped away. Now we seem to have come out on the other side, cleansed. Somehow the soul seems to stand up and take the light, naked and glorious.

Twice more we are to suffer through tragedies of Sophocles this day. Ah, but we shall welcome them. We await, content.

Oedipus Endures the Test of Time

Charles R. Walker

In 1966, the noted theatrical scholar and translator
Charles R. Walker published his fine, highly readable translations of Sophocles' *Oedipus the King* and
Oedipus at Colonus. In his introduction to the translations, Walker presents a detailed overview of how,
through the ages, succeeding generations of both
play producers and playgoers have repeatedly been
drawn to the character of Oedipus and to the tor-
tured events of his timeless story. In the following
excerpt, we learn how Sophocles' immediate Greek
successors viewed the play, how their enthusiasm
infected Roman playwrights and audiences, when
and where the first modern productions of Oedipus's
story took place, and how and why, despite the great
age of the material, interest in staging and watching
productions of it exploded in the second half of the
twentieth century.

If it were possible to count all the performances of *Oedipus
the King* since its first showing at the theater of Dionysus on
the side of the Acropolis in 429 B.C., it would undoubtedly
emerge as the most continuously produced play in dramatic
history. As to its reputation as a masterpiece—not to mention
the ink spent to explain it—it competes with [Shakespeare's]
Hamlet. But something quite new has happened to *Oedipus,*
as theater, since the Second World War. This ancient story of
incest and murder is now known, because of Freud and the
"Oedipus complex," to millions of men and women in the
modern world. Familiarity with the outline of the story,
however, is, at most, only a contributory cause to the tri-
umphal re-entry of Sophocles' play into the theaters of Europe, England, and the United States. . . . I have been con-

vinced that *Oedipus* and other Greek plays have begun to speak to the modern world with the authority of living theater. How and why has this happened?

Oedipus the King, aside from its subtleties of poetry and theme, is, of course, superb theater. It has the kind of hard, bony structure that can withstand almost any degree of bad direction and acting. But there are elements other than sheer theatrical effectiveness which account for its power. These relate to the mythical material out of which Sophocles and other ancient dramatists constructed their plays, material which has continued to attract writers up to the present day.

Here, however, we shall be concerned chiefly with *Oedipus* as theater, past and present. . . .

MARCHING THROUGH THE CENTURIES

Sophocles wrote *Oedipus the King* at the height of his career as a dramatist. Although Aristotle, a century later, chose it as the masterpiece of Greek tragedy, this most durable of Greek plays did not, at its initial showing, receive first prize. We know that Sophocles wrote what might be called the last act of the Oedipus drama, *Oedipus at Colonus*, years later. I shall argue that *Oedipus the King* needs this last act and that, in terms of both theater and the underlying myth, the two plays should be performed together to be fully understood.

After the great period of Greek drama the Oedipus story continued to march vigorously through the centuries. Talented actors in all ages have been especially attracted to the role of Oedipus. Polus, for example, the most famous actor of the fourth century, was especially renowned for his performances in both *Oedipus the King* and *Oedipus at Colonus*. During the fourth century B.C. the level of dramatic writing had declined, while the art of acting and the importance of individual actors rose. In fact, as actors became more influential they tended to modify classical dramas in order to give themselves more attractive roles. Finally Lycurgus, who was famous for rebuilding the theater of Dionysus and for his patronage of the ancient drama, put a stop to this tampering with Athens' classical heritage by ordering that state copies of all the tragedies be deposited in the archives and that a fine be imposed on anyone who changed the scripts. . . .

Greece fell under Roman rule in 146 B.C., but the Greek theater maintained a quasi-independence and enjoyed immense popularity throughout the empire well into the second century A.D. From what records we have of Roman productions, the story of Oedipus—in Sophocles' version as well as others—continued an active life in the theater of the Graeco-Roman world for another four hundred years. Classical scholars are fond of noting that Julius Caesar as a young man tried his hand as a playwright and wrote his own *Oedipus Rex.* The Emperor Nero acted Oedipus in a production of the Sophoclean play, and Seneca wrote a very dull but influential *Oedipus Rex.* Though Seneca introduced as much gore as might be expected from a gladiatorial combat, he managed to produce at the same time the least dramatic of all the extant [surviving] versions.

In the so-called Dark Ages, Greek tragedies faded from the consciousness of the West, although they continued to be performed for several centuries in the Byzantine Empire. A fragment of a bas-relief in the Hermitage, circa A.D. 500, shows scenes from *Medea* and *Oedipus*, and there are records of other performances to the end of the seventh century.

Early in the fifteenth century, Greek tragedies in manuscript began to reach Italy—brought by adventurous scholars from Byzantium. The most famous of these scholars, Giovanni Aurispa, literally sold the clothes off his back in Constantinople in order to bring back to Venice a booty of two hundred and thirty-eight manuscripts, including six tragedies of Aeschylus and seven of Sophocles. These tragedians as well as Euripides were edited and printed by Aldus, the Venetian scholar and Hellenist [enthusiast of Greek culture]. Sophocles was the first to be published, in 1502.

LAUNCHED IN THE MODERN THEATER

The modern theatrical life of *Oedipus the King* may be said to have begun rather precisely in Vicenza on March 3, 1585, when the Sophoclean tragedy was performed amid much pomp at the opening of the famous Teatro Olimpico of Palladio. The play was presented in an admirable Italian translation by the Venetian scholar and statesman Orsatto Giustiniani, with music by Andrea Gabrieli, organist at the Cathedral of San Marco. "It was fitting," wrote Filippo Pigafetta, a member of the first audience, "that this most renowned theater in the world should have as its first presentation the most excellent tragedy in the world.". . .

With the 1585 Vicenza performance, *Oedipus* was launched in the modern theater. Later, in the classical period of the

French theater, Corneille wrote his own version, adding a love plot. Racine considered competing with Sophocles, but refrained. Voltaire wrote an *Oedipe*, turning the play into an anticlerical tract, with the prophet Tiresias a venal and corrupt priest. . . .

In England, Dryden and Lee wrote a translation of Sophocles' *Oedipus*, effectively bowdlerizing [removing and censoring] all the shocking elements of the plot. Only in the nineteenth century, however, did *Oedipus* really begin his return to the modern theater—in preparation, it might be said, for something far more explosive and significant in the twentieth century. Performances in ancient Greek began to multiply in the universities in the middle of the nineteenth century and have continued up to the present day. There were many notable performances in the United States, in England, and on the Continent. Sir Richard Jebb, greatest of English Sophoclean scholars, crossed the Atlantic in 1888 to see the play given at Harvard. He includes an account of it in his famous—and still the best—edition of the play. Whether in the original or in the vernacular [translations], these performances in the theater introduced a new idea of Greek plays, an idea which seemed revolutionary and positively subversive to some classical scholars: that *Oedipus* and other Greek plays could only be fully understood in the theater, not in the library! The idea is still scorned by a dwindling number of regressive classicists. As part of this modernization movement, translations appeared in more or less speakable versions, often to the horror of the purely philological [those obsessed with the original wording].

Perhaps the two most famous productions of *Oedipus* in the late nineteenth and early twentieth centuries were those of the great French actor Mounet-Sully and of the German producer Max Reinhardt. Members of the audience who saw his performance say that Mounet-Sully's Oedipus was the greatest theatrical experience of their lives. In a generation when great actors played all the leading roles in the classics, from Shakespeare to Ibsen, Mounet-Sully believed his Oedipus to be (and he is supported by the testimony of contemporary critics) his greatest role. Mounet-Sully's first performance of *Oedipus* took place in a Roman amphitheater in the south of France; he was to play that role for many years, well into the twentieth century. He even made a silent movie of the play, without cutting the original.

Reinhardt's *Oedipus* exploded on the scene in 1910 in the Circus Schumann in Berlin, and again in 1919 in the gigantic Grosse Schulspielhaus. Though it used a German translation of Sophocles' text, the production was sheer Reinhardt, a mighty spectacle, complete with milling crowds and fervent realism in scenic and sound effects. Later, Reinhardt brought his production to England.

One theatergoer who was present at both the Mounet-Sully and the Reinhardt productions was J.T. Sheppard, the distinguished Greek scholar, then a young man and fellow of King's College, Cambridge. His comments were obviously written out of emotion, and with ideas that came to him in the theater and not in his Cambridge study.

Of Reinhardt's production he wrote: "That performance taught me that the strength of the plot makes the play great and exciting even in the worst conditions that a bad producer can invent."

Of Mounet-Sully's performance, which he saw in Paris, he said: "Because of its formal beauty, the French production is an inspiration to all who care for drama, and a proof that Greek drama, not bolstered up by sensationalism and with sentimentality, has power to hold and to move a modern audience. If you doubt whether in these days Greek tragedy still matters, you may learn the answer in Paris.". . .

A TOWERING PRODUCTION

The real *Oedipus* explosion, however, both in translation and performance, came only after the Second World War. Popular reading of Greek tragedy in translation has increased prodigiously in all Western countries. . . . In number of translations and in number of readers the English language leads all the rest, although excellent new versions are appearing in French, Italian, and modern Greek. . . .

[An] example of a towering modern production is that of Minotis and the Greek National Theater. Alexis Minotis has directed and acted in *Oedipus the King* in Greece, in the United States, in France, in Italy, and at the Edinburgh Theater festival. But it is only at the ancient Greek theater at Epidaurus that one can fully experience Minotis' *Oedipus.*

To begin with, the setting is dramatic and beautiful: fifty-five tiers of seats rise against Mt. Kynortion and look out over an expanse of tall cypresses and olive groves, where lie the ruins of a temple to Aesculapius and a vast complex of other buildings devoted to his cult and the cure of the sick. Epidaurus is famous for having the best-preserved round orchestra of any of the theaters of antiquity. In the center is the stone "thymele," or altar, which even today no Greek actor dare desecrate by stepping on. A two-story stage has been reconstructed on the far side, where most of the dialogue is spoken. The audience gathers slowly; there are tourists from abroad, but they lose themselves in the crowd. Front-row seats are reserved, as in Sophocles' time, for Greek and foreign dignitaries, but Greeks of all classes arrive in big American-built cars and in ramshackle local buses. Peasant women in black skirts with white kerchiefs round their heads come with their mustached men. They climb the fifty-five tiers to the cheaper seats, but the miraculous acoustics of the theater bring every word of the play even to those in the last rows. . . .

Here are a few of my impressions of Minotis' production, based on what I wrote down immediately after:

"Unimaginable force and fury in Oedipus' drive for the secret which he knows will mean his destruction. You see it causing him to threaten the old herdsman, first with words and then with physical pain. The shepherd's crook falls clattering to the ground and he begins to speak. . . .

"As the herdsman approaches the final telling, Oedipus goes behind the old man and tensely seizes his shoulders. Suddenly all difference in age, education, and rank between king and slave fall away; they become one in the terrible bond of their secret. In the last speech, revealing Oedipus' fate, the old man slowly reaches back and puts one hand on the hand of Oedipus, the man whom he has saved from death—yet for the most terrible of human destinies. Then a great cry from Oedipus—like a sword thrust—and the unforgettable speech, 'All true, all clear . . .'

"The final scene of the play, when Oedipus enters blinded—a scene that so many translators . . . have declared is too horrible to be borne by a modern audience—is the most absorbing and somehow the most satisfying in the whole tragedy. Here the audience seems wholly to lose itself in the counterpoint of Oedipus' emotions and in the purgation of pity and terror which they share with him."

APPEALING TO MODERN HOPES AND FEARS

So much for a compressed record of twenty-five centuries of *Oedipus the King.* What accounts for this remarkable durability? And what explains the return of *Oedipus* with renewed vigor into the theatrical world of the twentieth century?

Dramatic critics, from Aristotle on, have celebrated the uncanny ingenuity displayed by Sophocles in articulating his plots. And this surely is one reason for the *Oedipus* vitality. Shakespeare's plays have often been praised for their range of theatrical appeal, from pit to gallery. Whatever its other dimensions, the *Oedipus* of Sophocles may be enjoyed by the pit as a great whodunit whose plot exhibits great ingenuity in combining a maximum of horror and suspense as the protagonist tracks down the murderer. As to the play's architecture, scholars and critics have always admired its dramatic virtuosity and power. And in recent years the sharper psychological tools of modern criticism have added new levels of meaning as critics have sought to explore the depths of the ancient myth and Sophocles' treatment of it. . . .

More important than the superb plot—or, rather, inseparable from it—is the dynamism of the Sophoclean theme imbedded in it. As in *Hamlet*, men have always found half a dozen "universal" themes emerging from the play. To some of those in *Oedipus*, I would argue, the modern world is particularly responsive—a statement, incidentally, which applies to more than one Greek tragedy. In this play we are in the presence of a complex appeal—and challenge—to both the hopes and fears of modern man.

Who am I? Man searches for himself. What makes that eternal theme so penetrating and, in certain ways, so new to us in Sophocles' play? The key lies, I think, in certain curiously modern characteristics in Oedipus' personality and in his relation to his world. The reader may ask: What about those oracles, prophecies, gods, curses, pollutions, and all the other antique apparatus of the story? They certainly are not modern. No, but they melt somehow into credibility when seen through a supremely modern personality. Oedipus is a man of action, a successful leader with superior intelligence, possessed of extraordinary courage both physical and moral. However, if this were all, he would not interest us. Oedipus is an activist, but not an extrovert. His struggle for self-knowledge—and for mastery over his fears—is his passion and his destiny. One of his traits isn't common among us—to seek the truth at all costs—but the greatest scientists have taught us to admire such fortitude. From his first to his last appearance on the stage, Oedipus is presented by Sophocles as a man buffeted between the deductions of his admirable intellect and a whole psychological showcase of unconscious fears. Most of the latter are so deeply imbedded that only the most traumatic events can summon them to the surface of consciousness and make them live for us dramatically. But Sophocles summons them all. . . . There are two parallel plots in *Oedipus the King*, as all great actors playing the role of Oedipus have perceived: the plot of the hidden emotions rising from a graded series of unconscious depths and the defendant-prosecutor plot of external events. The interpenetration [fusing together] of the two, masterfully achieved, is what makes the play great—and new.

A Great Translator's Reflections on *Oedipus the King*

Gilbert Murray

In 1911, Gilbert Murray, a professor of Greek at Oxford University in England and one of the great classical scholars of the twentieth century, published his translation of Sophocles' *Oedipus the King*. In the preface, which appears here, Murray explains some of the qualities of the play that had drawn him to translate it, including, as he saw it, the compelling primitiveness of the story, the magnificence of the plot, and the great depth of the characterization. He also expresses what he apparently considered his own inadequacies as a translator, which, in looking back on the enormous contributions he made to modern interpretation of the Greek classics, now seems overly modest and certainly unwarranted. This document is revealing not only for its glimpse into the mind of a great Sophoclean translator but also for its analysis of Oedipus without reference to the ideas of psychoanalyst Sigmund Freud, who formally presented the concept of the Oedipus complex two years later.

If I have ... attempted a translation of the great stage masterpiece of Sophocles, my excuse must be the fascination of this play, which has thrown its spell on me as on many other translators. Yet I may plead also that as a rule every diligent student of these great works can add something to the discoveries of his predecessors, and I think I have been able to bring out a few new points in the old and much-studied *Oedipus*, chiefly points connected with the dramatic technique and the religious atmosphere.

Mythologists tell us that Oedipus was originally a [spirit]

From the translator's preface to Sophocles, *Oedipus, King of Thebes*, translated by Gilbert Murray (New York: Oxford University Press, 1911).

haunting Mount Kithairon [near Athens], and Jocasta a form of that Earth-Mother who, as Aeschylus puts it, "bringeth all things to being, and when she hath reared them receiveth again their seed into her body." That [very ancient] stage of the story lies very far behind the consciousness of Sophocles. But there does cling about both his hero and his heroine a great deal of very primitive atmosphere. There are traces in Oedipus of the pre-hellenic Medicine King, [who] can make rain or blue sky, pestilence or fertility. This explains many things in the Priest's first speech, in the attitude of the Chorus, and in Oedipus' own language after the discovery [of his true identity]. . . .

The story itself, and the whole spirit in which Sophocles has treated it, belong not to the fifth century [B.C.] but to that terrible and romantic past from which the fifth century poets usually drew their material. The atmosphere of brooding dread, the pollution, the curses; the "insane and beast-like cruelty," as an ancient Greek commentator calls it, of piercing the exposed child's feet in order to ensure its death and yet avoid having actually murdered it; the whole treatment of the parricide and incest, not as moral offences capable of being rationally judged or even excused as unintentional, but as monstrous and inhuman pollutions, the last limit of imaginable horror: all these things take us back to dark regions of pre-classical and even pre-homeric [before Homer's time] belief. We have no right to suppose that Sophocles thought of the involuntary parricide . . . as the people in his play do. Indeed, considering the general tone of his contemporaries and friends, we may safely assume that he did not. But at any rate he has allowed no breath of later enlightenment to disturb the primaeval [primitive] gloom of his atmosphere.

Does this in any way make the tragedy insincere? I think not. We know that people did feel and think about "pollution" in the way which Sophocles represents; and if they so felt, then the tragedy was there.

AMAZING GRANDEUR AND POWER

I think these considerations explain the remarkable absence from this play of any criticism of life or any definite moral judgment. I know that some commentators have found in it a " humble and unquestioning piety," but I cannot help suspecting that what they saw was only a reflection from their own pious and unquestioning minds. Man is indeed shown as a "plaything of Gods," but of Gods strangely and incomprehensibly malignant [mean-spirited], whose ways there is no attempt to explain or justify. The original story, indeed, may have had one of its roots in a Theban "moral tale." Aelian [an ancient Roman writer who studied Greek myths and customs] tells us that the exposure [leaving outside to die] of a child was forbidden by Theban Law. The state of feeling which produced this law, against the immensely strong conception of the *patria potestas* [traditional power of the father over members of the household], may also have produced a folklore story telling how a boy once was exposed, in a peculiarly cruel way, by his wicked parents, and how Heaven preserved him to take upon both of them a vengeance which showed that the unnatural father had no longer a father's sanctity nor the unnatural mother a mother's. But, as far as Sophocles is concerned, if anything in the nature of a criticism of life has been admitted into the play at all, it seems to be only a flash or two. . . .

There is not much philosophy in the *Oedipus*. There is not, in comparison with other Greek plays, much pure poetry. What there is, is drama; drama of amazing grandeur and power. In respect of plot no Greek play comes near it. It contains no doubt a few points of unsophisticated technique such as can be found in all ancient and nearly all modern drama; for instance, the supposition that Oedipus has never inquired into the death of his predecessor on the throne. But such flaws are external, not essential. On the whole, I can only say that the work of translation has made me feel even more strongly than before the extraordinary grip and reality of the dialogue, the deftness of the construction, and . . . the unbroken crescendo of tragedy from the opening to the close.

CHARACTERS VITAL AND DISTINCT

Where plot-interest is as strong as it is in the *Oedipus*, character-interest is apt to be comparatively weak. Yet in this play every character is interesting, vital, and distinct. Oedipus himself is selected by Aristotle as the most effective kind of tragic hero, because, first, he has been great and glorious, and secondly he has not been "pre-eminently virtuous or just." This is true in its way. Oedipus is too passionate to be just; but he is at least noble in his impetuosity, his devotion, and his absolute truthfulness. It is important to realise that at the beginning of the play he is prepared for an oracle commanding him to die for his people. And he never thinks of refusing that "task" any more than he tries to elude the doom that actually comes, or to conceal any fact that tells against him. If Oedipus had been an ordinary man the play would have been a very different and a much poorer thing.

TIRESIAS'S DIRE PREDICTION

In this speech excerpted from Oedipus the King, *the priest Tiresias informs Oedipus that Laius's killer stands before him and predicts that the murderer will eventually be reduced to a blind beggar. It is an example of the highly dramatic qualities of the priest's character.*

> TIRESIAS (*turning again as he goes*).
> I fear you not; nor will I go before
> That word be spoken which I came to speak.
> How can you ever touch me?—You do seek
> With threats and loud proclaim the man whose hand
> Slew Laïus. Lo, I tell you, he does stand
> Here. He is called a stranger, but these days
> Shall prove him Theban true, nor shall he praise
> His birthright. Blind, who once had seeing eyes,
> Beggared, who once had riches, in strange guise,
> His staff groping before him, he shall crawl
> O'er unknown earth, and voices round him call:
> "Behold the brother-father of his own
> Children, the seed, the sower and the sown,
> Shame to his mother's blood, and to his sire
> Son, murderer, incest-worker."
>   Cool your ire
> With thought of these, and if you find that
> Fails, then hold my craft a thing of naught [useless].

Jocasta is a wonderful study. Euripides [in his own version of the legend] might have brought her character out more explicitly and more at length, but even he could not have made her more living or more tragic, or represented more subtly in her relation to Oedipus both the mother's protecting love and the mother's authority. As for her "impiety," of which the old commentaries used to speak with much disapproval, the essential fact in her life is that both her innocence and her happiness have, as she believes, been poisoned by the craft of priests. She and Laïus both "believed a bad oracle": her terror and her love for her husband made her consent to an infamous act of cruelty to her own child, an act of which the thought sickens her still, and about which she cannot, when she tries, speak the whole truth. And after all her crime was for nothing! The oracle proved to be a lie. Never again will she believe a priest.

As to Tiresias . . . [he] is a study of a real type, and a type which all the tragedians knew. The character of the professional seer or "man of God" has in the imagination of most ages fluctuated between two poles. At one extreme are sanctity [holiness] and superhuman wisdom; at the other fraud and mental disease, self-worship aping humility and personal malignity [hatred or malice] in the guise of obedience to God. There is a touch of all these qualities, good and bad alike, in Tiresias. He seems to me a most life-like as well as a most dramatic figure.

BLURRING THE OUTLINES

As to the Chorus, it generally plays a smaller part in Sophocles than in Euripides and Aeschylus, and the Oedipus forms no exception to that rule. It seems to me that Sophocles was feeling his way towards a technique which would have approached that of the [later Greek] New Comedy or even the Elizabethan [Shakespearean] stage, and would perhaps have done without a Chorus altogether. In Aeschylus Greek tragedy had been a thing of traditional forms and clear-cut divisions; the religious ritual showed through, and the visible gods and the disguised dancers were allowed their full value. And Euripides in the matter of outward formalism went back to the Aeschylean type and even beyond it: prologue, chorus, messenger, visible god, all the traditional forms were left clear-cut and undisguised and all developed to full effectiveness on separate and specific lines. But Sophocles worked by blurring his structural outlines just as he blurs the ends of his verses. In him the traditional divisions are all made less distinct, all worked over in the direction of greater naturalness. . . . This was a very great gain, but of course some price had to be paid for it. Part of the price was that Sophocles could never attempt the tremendous choric effects which Euripides achieves in such plays as the *Bacchae* and the *Trojan Women.* His lyrics, great as they sometimes are, move their wings less boldly. They seem somehow tied to their particular place in the tragedy, and they have not quite the strength to lift the whole drama bodily aloft with them. . . . At least that is my feeling. But I realise that this may be only the complaint of an unskilful translator, blaming his material for his own defects of vision.

In general, both in lyrics and in dialogue, I believe I have allowed myself rather less freedom than in translating Euripides. This is partly because . . . there is in Sophocles, amid all his passion and all his naturalness, a certain severe and classic reticence [reserve and restraint].

The Oedipus Complex: A Theory Under Fire

Bruce Bower

In the first years of the twentieth century, the respected Austrian psychoanalyst Sigmund Freud proposed his controversial theory that early childhood
and family relationships are driven to a large extent
by repressed sexual urges, particularly that of little
boys for their mothers. Because the concept was
based in large degree on the characters and plot of
Sophocles' *Oedipus the King*, it became popularly
known as the Oedipus complex. This theory became
one of the cornerstones of modern psychoanalysis
and helped earn Freud the unofficial title of father of
that field. In recent years, however, as behavioral
science writer Bruce Bower explains, *Oedipus Rex*
has become Oedipus "wrecked" in the wake of criticisms leveled by modern psychologists who have increasingly taken exception to Freud's famous theory.

Poor Oedipus Rex. Twice he has achieved royal status, only
to have the red carpet rudely pulled out from under him.
First, as described in a play written by the 5th century B.C.
Greek dramatist Sophocles, Oedipus triumphantly ascended
to the throne of ancient Thebes. Master of all he surveyed,
the new king then hit rock bottom. Upon learning that he
had unwittingly killed his father and married his mother,
Oedipus gouged out his own eyes.

Much later, Sigmund Freud honored the tragic king by
dubbing the central theory of psychoanalysis the Oedipus
complex. Freud proposed that all toddlers direct their first
sexual longings at the opposite-sex parent and consequently
aim their first feelings of intense rivalry toward the same-
sex parent. Healthy psychological development requires a
resolution and redirection of these urges, the Viennese psy-

Bruce Bower, "Oedipus Wrecked," *Science News*, October 19, 1991. Reprinted with permission of *Science News*, the weekly newsmagazine of science; copyright 1991 by Science Service, Inc.

chiatrist asserted. Dressed in his Freudian finery, Oedipus strutted into the 20th century and seized the imaginations of psychoanalysts, social scientists, artists, writers and other observers of the human condition.

Now, however, the Oedipus complex shows its own flair for tragedy, as it falls from grace among many of Freud's intellectual progeny [offspring] and faces empirical challenges from psychologists and other researchers influenced by Charles Darwin's theory of evolution.

"The Oedipus complex clearly has waned in popularity and credibility, both within psychoanalysis and within the culture at large," contends psychiatrist Bennett Simon of Harvard Medical School in Boston. Simon describes psychoanalytic "confusion and disagreement" over the Oedipus complex in the July–September [1991] *Journal of the American Psychoanalytic Association.*

Evolutionary psychologists and anthropologists, who view social behavior as the outgrowth of evolution by natural selection, generally respect Freud's intellectual contributions but consider the Oedipus complex a misguided explanation of conflict between parents and children. Natural selection—the preservation in a species of genetically based traits that best contribute to the survival and reproduction of individuals and their genetic relatives—has produced typical forms of parent-child conflict that have nothing to do with incestuous desires, according to evolutionary investigators.

OEDIPAL MOVERS AND SHAKERS

The Oedipus complex produced unease and dissension among psychoanalysts almost from the start, Simon points out. Freud first laid out the basis of the theory—without mentioning Oedipus by name—in *The Interpretation of Dreams* in 1900. He then elaborated the concept in works such as *Totem and Taboo* (1913), in which he proposed that the little boy's urge to kill his father and mate with his mother stemmed from one or more incidents of actual father murder carried out by Stone Age men. Ancient homicides of fathers by sons—an idea since rejected by anthropologists—ushered in incest taboos, religion and culture, Freud argued.

In perhaps his most controversial Oedipal formulation, Freud described different paths of healthy sexual and moral development for girls and boys. Oedipal urges lead to castration anxieties in boys, who then resolve the dilemma by turning to the father for moral and religious guidance, resulting in a strong "superego," or conscience, he maintained. Freud made no secret of his difficulty in explaining female development, but suggested that girls experience penis envy, which creates anger at the mother and a subsequent turn to the father. Without the intense unconscious push males get from Oedipally derived castration fears, the female superego ends up weaker than that of males, Freud posited [proposed].

IN FREUD'S OWN WORDS

Sigmund Freud briefly describes an aspect of the Oedipus complex in this excerpt from his lecture "Anxiety and Instinctual Life," first given in the winter of 1916–1917.

We have recently been examining the way in which anxiety is generated in certain phobias which we class as anxiety hysteria, and have chosen cases in which we were dealing with the typical repression of wishful impulses arising from the Oedipus complex. We should have expected to find that it was a libidinal cathexis of [sexual attachment to] the boy's mother as object which, as a result of repression, had been changed into anxiety and which now emerged, expressed in symptomatic terms, attached to a substitute for his father. I cannot present you with the detailed steps of an investigation such as this; it will be enough to say that the surprising result was the opposite of what we expected. It was not the repression that created the anxiety; the anxiety was there earlier; it was the anxiety that made the repression.

By the late 1920s, some prominent psychoanalysts questioned the alleged inferiority of the female conscience and downplayed the role assigned to the Oedipal complex. Freud's closest protégé, Otto Rank, noted the "anti-Oedipal" tendency displayed by children trying to keep their parents together when divorce loomed, and cautioned against the rigid application of the Oedipus complex to individual patients. One current school of psychoanalytic thought rejects Freud's assertion that the Oedipus complex occurs universally, arguing instead that psychologically disturbed parents sometimes stir up incestuous and intensely competitive feelings in their children.

Other psychoanalysts cast off conflict and sexuality as the prime Oedipal movers and shakers. For instance, psychiatrist E. James Lieberman of George Washington University School of Medicine in Washington, D.C., contends that Sophocles' *Oedipus Rex* emphasizes themes of family love and altruism, not the hostility and fear described by Freud. In the play, Oedipus grew up with adoptive parents whom he dearly loved, and only left them when told of his incestuous and homicidal fate by an oracle, Lieberman observes. At the time of his departure, Oedipus did not know that the oracle's prophecy referred to his biological parents.

"Legal or biological paternity needs a human relationship to give it significance," Lieberman writes in the June [1991] *Harvard Mental Health Letter.* "Oedipus really loved his [adoptive] father. The moral of the drama is that honest, loving family ties are the best defense against dire prophecy and the greatest security in an uncertain world."

FATHER-SON RIVALRIES

True enough, respond evolutionary theorists, but mounting evidence indicates that even loving parents and their children encounter important conflicts that fall outside the realm of incestuous desire. Two theories guide the evolutionary approach. The first, proposed by Finnish anthropologist Edward Westermarck in 1891, holds that natural selection has endowed humans and other animals with an unconscious mental tendency to avoid inbreeding and its harmful genetic effects on offspring. This mental "adaptation" automatically motivates sexual avoidance among individuals raised together in the same family or group, regardless of the degree to which their genetic backgrounds match, Westermarck argued.

A second model, developed since 1974 by Harvard University sociobiologist Robert L. Trivers and several others, maintains that natural selection has produced children, daughters and sons alike, who generally covet more attention, help and other resources than parents—and mothers in particular—reasonably can offer, especially as additional offspring enter the family. The result: occasional parent-child friction and sibling rivalries even in the most tranquil families.

An analysis of homicides within families fits the Darwinian perspective better than Freud's Oedipal scenario of childhood rivalry with the same-sex parent, report Canadian psychologists Martin Daly and Margo Wilson, both of McMaster University in Hamilton, Ontario, in the March 1990 *Journal of Personality.* Their review of all reported murders of children by their parents and all murders of parents by their children in Canada between 1974 and 1983, and in Chicago between 1965 and 1981, finds no evidence of a same-sex bias in killings of children during the Oedipal phase (ages 2 to 5). Whether the mother or father committed the murder, the proportion of male to female victims remains nearly even. And no evidence of same-sex bias in the physical abuse of young children by mothers versus fathers turns up either, the researchers observe.

At all ages except during the Oedipal years, sons outnumber daughters as murder victims, more often at the hands of their fathers, Daly and Wilson note. Impoverished parents make up the bulk of child murderers, they add.

Adolescent boys display the greatest likelihood of murdering a parent, particularly the father. This trend probably reflects rivalries over the use and control of family property, Daly and Wilson suggest.

Freud collapsed two distinct father-son rivalries into one, the two psychologists conclude: an early conflict over access to the mother that does not involve sexual rivalry, and a later rivalry during adolescence—often seen in nonindustrial, polygynous societies—involving competition for women other than the mother or the control of family wealth.

SOCIAL TABOOS

Freud—and many scholars in his wake—also erred in assuming that all human societies retain explicit taboos against incest within the immediate family, contends anthropologist Nancy W. Thornhill of the University of New Mexico in Albuquerque. Incest rules primarily exist to regulate mating between in-laws and cousins rather than close genetic relatives, who show little interest in incest, Thornhill concludes in the June [1991] *Behavioral and Brain Sciences.*

Thornhill tracked information on mating and marriage rules in the ethnographies of 129 societies—from the 16th-century Incas to the 20th-century Vietnamese—stored at the Human Relations Area Files in New Haven, Conn., a research arm of Yale University. Only 57 of the societies—less than half—specified rules against nuclear family incest, whereas 114 societies designated rules to control mating or marriage with cousins, in-laws or both, Thornhill reports.

Rules regulating mating between in-laws serve as checks on paternity and obstacles to female adultery, mainly in the societies that require a woman to live with her husband and his relatives upon marriage, the New Mexico researcher argues. Only 14 of the ethnographies describe societies that require a man to live with his wife and her relatives upon marriage, and most of those societies either lack rules regarding in-law mating or mete out mild punishments for an infraction of the rules, she adds.

Rulers of stratified societies enforce sanctions against cousin marriage and inbreeding in order to secure their lofty positions by discouraging the concentration of wealth and power within families other than their own, Thornhill notes. In non-stratified societies, with no central rulers and relatively equal distribution of food and other resources, dictums [rules] against cousin unions foil the accumulation of wealth in extended families and maintain the level social playing field trod by most men, in her view.

A CAULDRON OF DECEPTION

In Thornhill's survey of worldwide societies, the more highly stratified the society, the more kin outside the immediate family fall under inbreeding regulations. However, rulers in stratified societies rarely observe those rules and frequently marry their own relatives—although they may not mate with them—in the quest to consolidate their power, Thornhill points out.

Although increasing reports in the United States and elsewhere of parent-child incest seem to demonstrate strong—indeed, sometimes overpowering—Oedipal urges within the nuclear family, appearances prove deceiving, according to Thornhill. In fact, data on incest cases tend to support Westermarck's theory, she says. For instance, studies in the United States and Canada find that step-fathers, not genetic fathers, most often initiate incest, and typically had no regular contact with a youthful victim during the first few years of the child's life. Reports of incest between genetic fathers and their daughters involve sexual intercourse far less often than incest between step-fathers and daughters, Thornhill says.

Sexual intercourse between close genetic relatives rarely occurs because natural selection has molded a human psyche that promotes paternity concerns in men and the striving for status and resource control through social competition in both sexes, Thornhill proposes. Cultural and moral taboos against incest sprang from these psychological foundations.

Psychoanalysts—psychiatrists and psychologists who undergo special clinical training and receive psychotherapy based on Freud's theories—remain largely ignorant of the evolutionary theories about family conflict, even as their enthusiasm for the Oedipus complex subsides, says psychologist Malcolm O. Slavin of Tufts University Counseling Center in Medford, Mass. Slavin, a trained psychoanalyst, uses an evolutionary perspective in his psychotherapy.

"Fathers and children engage in much competition and rivalry over the mother's scarce time and resources, even in loving families," Slavin asserts. "It's often hard for family members to reconcile this conflict with the love and support they give to one another."

Family conflict swirls in a cauldron of deception forged by natural selection, Slavin argues. Men who successfully seek additional or more desirable mates, and women who attract the best marriage prospects often employ deception to mislead same-sex competitors and maximize the deceiver's perceived attractiveness, he says. What's more, deception works best when the deceiver remains unaware of his or her true motives and cannot give the strategy away. Thus, according to Slavin, evolution has promoted the psychological repression, or unconscious stowing away, of disturbing thoughts, fantasies and selfish motives.

"We're never motivated to reveal ourselves fully to others or to ourselves," he maintains.

Minds That Can Endure Doubt

Some psychoanalytically oriented researchers, however, see no reason to discard Freud's theory of the Oedipus complex. They believe it works in concert with evolutionary tendencies to discourage incest.

Evolutionary or sociobiological theories address the reproductive concerns that have fostered incest avoidance in the human species, while psychoanalytic theory explains how individual development further blocks the possibility of incest, asserts anthropologist Robert A. Paul of Emory University in Atlanta. Freud argued that the child normally represses erotic feelings toward an opposite-sex parent or sibling out of fear of reprisal from the same-sex parent, Paul says. Freud's emphasis on the child's experience in the family and Westermarck's focus on natural selection provide complementary explanations of the rarity of incest, he remarks.

"The human superego is a powerful part of this 'incest avoidance complex,'" adds anthropologist David H. Spain of the University of Washington in Seattle. The largely unconscious influence of the child's emerging moral conscience as a result of Oedipal conflicts helps explain why most of the societies studied by Thornhill require no explicit incest taboos, Spain contends.

Thornhill disagrees. The traditional Freudian view assumes intense sexual attractions naturally occur among family members, while evolutionary theories present evidence of sexual repugnance among close genetic relatives, she says.

Freud, who considered his theories a preliminary step toward a scientific psychology, might extract a certain intellectual excitement from the debate surrounding the Oedipus complex. "Mediocre spirits demand of science the kind of certainty which it cannot give, a sort of religious satisfaction," he wrote to his friend Princess Marie Bonaparte toward the end of his life. "Only the real, rare, true scientific minds can endure doubt, which is attached to all our knowledge."

CHAPTER 3

Producing Sophocles' Plays

READINGS ON
SOPHOCLES

Ajax: Lonely Hero of a Bygone Age

Bernard M.W. Knox

For his play *Ajax*, Sophocles chose a story and characters very familiar to his Greek audiences—the legendary siege of the city of Troy by the Greek kings
and warriors of a bygone age. The Trojan War and
its heroes were the subjects of the epic poem the
Iliad, attributed to the equally legendary eighth-
century B.C. wandering poet, Homer. The playwright
chose to illuminate that portion of the Homeric story
in which Ajax is disappointed at not receiving the
armor of the slain Achilles, the mightiest of the
Greek warriors at the siege. Ajax, second only to
Achilles in strength and valor, is enraged that the
other generals have passed him over and voted to
award the armor to the wily Odysseus. This is the
source of Ajax's subsequent eternal hatred for
Odysseus. In this excerpt from his brilliant 1961
analysis of the play, renowned classical scholar
Bernard M.W. Knox argues that an understanding of
the story and the main character rests on the realization that Ajax, like the great and proud Achilles, was
part of a semimythical world in which love, hatred,
and other emotions were absolute and unchanging.
There, mighty, arrogant, and lonely warriors existed,
and in a sense will always exist, untouched by the
ravages of time.

The key to an understanding of this harsh and beautiful play
is the great speech in which Ajax debates his course of action and explores the nature of man's life on earth. These
lines are so majestic, remote, and mysterious, and at the
same time so passionate, dramatic, and complex, that if this
were all that had survived of Sophocles he would still have

Excerpts from Bernard M.W. Knox's "The Ajax of Sophocles," HARVARD STUDIES IN
CLASSICAL PHILOLOGY, LXV (1961), 1-37. Copyright ©1961 by the President and
Fellows of Harvard College. Reprinted with permission.

to be reckoned as one of the world's greatest poets. They are the point from which this discussion starts and to which it will return, for in the play all the poetic and thematic threads which make up the stark pattern of the *Ajax* start from and run back to this speech. These magnificent, enigmatic lines, alternately serene and passionate, and placed almost dead center in the action, offer us the only moment of repose and reflection in a play which begins in monstrous violence and hatred, and maintains that atmosphere almost unbroken to the end. . . .

Ajax is onstage in every scene, first alive, then dead. The rest of the characters follow him wherever he goes; Odysseus tracks him to his tent, and later Tecmessa and the chorus follow his tracks to the lonely place on the shore where he has killed himself. The hero's death, which normally in Attic tragedy is described by a messenger who accompanies the body onstage, takes place before our eyes in the *Ajax*, and to make this possible Sophocles has recourse to the rare and difficult expedient of changing the scene; when Ajax moves, the whole play follows after him. Further . . . the poetry of the play (and it contains some of Sophocles' most magnificent lines) is all assigned to Ajax. Brutal and limited he may be, but there can be no doubt that Sophocles saw him as heroic. The lamentations of Tecmessa, Teucer, and the chorus express our own sense of a great loss. The tone of the speeches made over his body in the second half of the play emphasizes the fact that the world is a smaller, meaner place because of his death. The last half of the play shows us a world emptied of greatness; all that was great in the world lies there dead, impaled on that gigantic sword, while smaller men, with motives both good and bad, dispute over its burial. The unheroic tone of the end of the play (with its threats and boasts and personal insults) has often been criticized as an artistic failure; surely it is deliberate. Nothing else would make us feel what has happened. A heroic age has passed away, to be succeeded by one in which action is replaced by argument, stubbornness by compromise, defiance by acceptance. The heroic self-assertion of an Achilles, an Ajax, will never be seen again; the best this new world has to offer is the humane and compromising temper of Odysseus, the worst the ruthless and cynical cruelty of the Atridae. But nothing like the greatness of the man who lies there dead. . . .

Ajax's assumption of godlike confidence is only an extreme expression of his fierce dedication to the traditional
morality. In pursuing the heroic code to the bloodthirsty and
megalomaniac extremes the prologue puts before us, he is
acting not like a man but like a god. "May Zeus grant me,"
sang that bitter and vengeful poet Theognis, "to repay my
friends who love me and my enemies who now triumph
over me, and I would seem to be a god among men." Ajax
acts and thinks like a god among men. Like a god he judges,
condemns, and executes his enemies, with speed, certainty,
and righteous wrath. The gods do indeed act like this, but
they can do so because they have knowledge. "Learn," says
Athena to Odysseus, "from one who knows." But man is ignorant. "We know nothing clear," says Odysseus. "We are
adrift." The same standard of conduct will not be valid for
man in his ignorance and gods in their knowledge. What is
wrong for one may be right for the other. . . .

TALKING TO HIMSELF

Ajax comes at last to his moment of unclouded vision, in
which he sees the world man lives in as it really is. He explores, for himself and for us, the nature of the ceaseless
change which is the pattern of the universe. The famous
speech in which he does so has caused a dispute among the
critics which is still alive; there are two main schools of
thought about it. One believes that the speech is a sincere re-
cantation of stubbornness, a decision to submit to authority,
human and divine, and so go on living. The other believes
that the speech is a disguised and ambiguous reassertion of
the hero's will for death, and though different critics of this
majority school differ in their estimates of how much of the
speech is sincere and how much not, they are all united on
the point that the speech is intended to deceive Tecmessa
and the chorus. . . .

Does Ajax intend to deceive his hearers, masking his un-
changed purpose, death, with ambiguous words? There can
be no doubt that he does deceive Tecmessa and his sailors;
Tecmessa later complains bitterly that she was "cast out
from his love and deceived." But does Ajax consciously and
deliberately deceive her and the chorus? If so, we are faced
with a problem as difficult as that raised by the other point
of view—a serious inconsistency of character. The character
of Ajax is Achillean [like Achilles]; it may be all too easily

AJAX'S LAMENT

This speech from Sophocles' play Ajax *forms the center of Knox's analysis.*

AJAX (*enters, sword in hand*). All things the long and countless years first draw from darkness, then bury from light; and there is nothing for which man may not look. The dread oath is vanquished, and the stubborn will. Even I, once so wonderfully firm, like iron hardened in the dipping, have felt the keen edge of my temper softened by yonder woman's words. I feel the pity of leaving her a widow with my foes and the boy an orphan.

But I will go to the bathing place and the meadows by the shore, that in purging of my stains I may flee the heavy anger of the goddess. Then I will seek out some untrodden spot and bury this sword, hatefulest of weapons, in a hole dug where none shall see; no, let Night and Hades keep it underground! For since my hand took this gift from Hector, my worst foe, to this hour I have had no good from the Greeks. Yes, men's proverb is true: "The gifts of enemies are no gifts and bring no good."

I shall henceforth know, therefore, how to yield to the gods and shall learn to revere the Atreidae. They are rulers, so we must submit. How else? Dread things and things most potent bow to office; thus it is that snow-strewn winter gives place to fruitful summer; and thus night's weary round makes room for day with her white steeds to kindle light; and the breath of dreadful winds can allow the groaning sea to slumber; and, like the rest, almighty Sleep looses whom he has bound, nor holds with a perpetual grasp.

And we—must we not learn discretion? I, at least, will learn it; for I am newly aware that our enemy is to be hated but as one who will hereafter be a friend; and toward a friend I would wish but thus far to show aid and service, as knowing that he will not always abide. For to most men the haven of friendship is false.

But concerning these things it will be well. Woman, go you within and pray to the gods that in all fullness the desires of my heart may be fulfilled. And you, my friends, do you honor these my wishes just as she does; and bid Teucer when he comes to have care for me and also good will toward you. For I will go whither I must pass, but you do my bidding. Before long, perhaps, though I am now suffering you will hear that I have found peace. (*Exit.*)

tempted to extremes of violence, but not to deceit. . . .

The idea that he would have to lie in order to escape from Tecmessa and his sailors is one that could never have occurred to Ajax. The intent to deceive is not only uncharacteristic of Ajax, it has no adequate motive in the dramatic circumstances.

All this merely replaces the dilemmas faced by previous critics with another dilemma, which appears to be equally insoluble. If Ajax is not trying to deceive Tecmessa and the chorus, masking an unbroken resolve for death with ambiguous phrases, and if he is not on the other hand trying to tell them, sincerely and without reservations, that he will make his peace with gods and men, and live, then what is he trying to tell them?

There is only one possible answer. He is not trying to tell them anything at all. He is talking to himself. During the first part of his speech he is oblivious of their presence, totally self-absorbed in an attempt to understand not only the nature of the world which has brought him to this pass but also the new feelings which rise in him and prompt him to reconsider his decision for death.

This solution of the difficulty, that the first thirty-nine lines of Ajax's speech are soliloquy [words spoken alone] and therefore rule out the question of his intentions toward Tecmessa and the chorus, is suggested by an unusual feature of the speech, which has not been given the attention it deserves. The speech comes directly after the closing lines of a choral stasimon, and thus opens the scene. But contrary to usual practice, it plunges abruptly into the philosophical reflections on time, without any form of address to the chorus or Tecmessa. In the theatre of Dionysos the vast size of the auditorium, the distance between even the closest spectators and the actors, and, above all, the masks excluded that play of facial expression which in the modern theater makes clear at once the direction of the actor's remarks; we can see, and do not have to be told, whom the actor is addressing. But the Athenian dramatist (and this was especially true of the opening moments of a new scene) felt obliged to establish firmly, clearly, and at once the relationship between the opening speaker and his dramatic audience. He put the opening speaker in some clear verbal rapport with the other person or persons on the stage or in the orchestra, by means of a choral introduction, a vocative formula, or a verb in the second person. But in this speech there is nothing whatsoever to indicate whom Ajax is talking to, nothing until the fortieth line of the speech.

THE WORLD OF TIME

Such an opening speech is almost unparalleled in Sophoclean tragedy. In fact there is only one parallel. It is in this same play, the *Ajax*; it is the last speech Ajax makes. And here of course the absence of verbal rapport with the others is easy to understand; there *are* no others, not even the chorus. Ajax is alone onstage.

The opening lines of the great speech on time give the impression that Ajax is talking to himself, just as he does later when he *is* alone. And that impression is maintained. For thirty-nine lines there is no indication that he is talking to anyone else, no vocative formula, no verb in the second person. . . .

The great speech of Ajax, for most of its length, is not meant for anyone but himself; since he is a character in a play, that means that it is meant exclusively for us, the audience. He is not trying to deceive, but to understand, to understand the nature of the world which once seemed (and was) so simple, but in which he has now lost his way, to understand what his place is in this new-found, complicated world, and to decide on his next step. . . .

The great speech of Ajax defines the world of time which is man's place and illustrates the impracticality of the traditional code. But it does something more. It discusses the plight of man, time's subject, not only in terms of his relation to gods and his private relation to other men, friends and enemies, but also in terms of his relation to the community. The dilemma of Ajax illuminates not only the metaphysical and moral aspects of man's life on earth, but also the political and social.

DEATH OF A HEROIC AGE

Ajax is presented to us in this play as the last of the heroes. His death is the death of the old Homeric (and especially Achillean) individual ethos which had for centuries of aristocratic rule served as the dominant ideal of man's nobility and action, but which by the fifth century had been successfully challenged and largely superseded . . . by an outlook more suitable to the conditions of the polis [community of the city-state], an outlook which reached its most developed form in democratic Athens. Ajax is presented to us throughout in terms of this heroic morality; this is the function of the wealth of Homeric reminiscence which editors have noted in the language of the play. The words used by Ajax and about him recall the epic atmosphere of the heroic age, and since many of these words are spoken by his enemies, we are shown a full critique of the ideal, its greatness and also its limitations. . . .

Ajax, like Achilles before him, is a law unto himself; his ideal is the Homeric one: "always to be best, and superior to the others." The virtues demanded of a man in a society of equals—tolerance, adaptability, persuasiveness—have no place in his make-up. . . .

Ajax is indeed unfit for the new age, the political institutions which impose rotation and cession of power, which recognize and encourage change. . . .

Ajax belongs to a world which for Sophocles and his audience had passed away—an aristocratic, heroic, half-mythic world which had its limitations but also its greatness, a world in which father was like son and nothing ever changed, in which great friendships, and also great hatreds, endured forever.

But in the world as Ajax has at last come to see it, nothing remains forever. . . .

Ajax's defiance of time and its imperative of change consists not in his suicide (which was in any case his only way of escape from ignominious death) but in his final reassertion of hatred, his passionate vindication of the old heroic code. The problem which faces Ajax is not whether to live or to die, for die he must, but in what mood to die. He dies, as he had lived, hating his enemies. He does not know, and we are made to feel that he would not want to know, that his most hated enemy, Odysseus, will champion his cause against the Atridae. He would rather die than have to recognize Odysseus as a friend. He dies to perpetuate his hatred. His last fierce, vengeful, and beautiful speech is an attempt to arrest, for one man at least, the ebb and flow of relationship between man and man; he may be utterly alone, but he at least will hate his enemies forever.

His brother Teucer understands this. That is why he will not let Odysseus take part in the burial of Ajax. Ajax killed himself to defy a world in which he might one day have to help or feel gratitude to Odysseus. "I shrink from letting you put your hands on his body to help bury him. I am afraid it would offend the dead man." Teucer is right, of course. Ajax hates Odysseus more than any other man. And these words of Teucer remind us, as they must have reminded and were doubtless meant to remind the Athenian audience, of Odysseus' own account, in Homer [in the *Odyssey*], of his meeting with the shade [spirit] of Ajax in the lower world: "Only the shade of Ajax ... stood apart in anger ... 'Ajax,' I said, 'so you were not going to forget your anger against me, even in death ... Come here to me, my lord, hear what I have to say. Subdue your pride and noble spirit.' So I spoke to him. He made no answer, but strode off after the other shades to the dark house of the dead and gone.". . . This is the permanence Ajax has chosen. It is an eternity of hatred and loneliness, but it is the permanence he longed for—he will hate always, forgive never. His yearning for the absolute, the permanent, is fulfilled by his everlasting existence as a proud and silent hater of his enemy, alone, but free, free of the shifting pattern of constant change, free of time.

Sophocles Is Interpreted in Black Gospel Music

Mimi Kramer

In this theater review written in the spring of 1988, *New Yorker* magazine drama critic Mimi Kramer comments on both the text and presentation of *The Gospel at Colonus*, a stage production that retold Sophocles' classic play *Oedipus at Colonus* using modern black gospel music and idioms. Kramer contends that this drastic updating and change of style worked well, partly because the original play explores themes such as suffering, sin, and redemption, which are also common to Christianity and the black experience. In particular, she states, the people of fifth-century B.C. Athens, for whom Sophocles wrote his plays, were strongly preoccupied with and motivated by the same primary values that underlie gospel music—church and family.

Oedipus at Colonus was Sophocles' last play, his love song to Periclean Athens. Written in the closing years of the fifth century B.C., when Athens was losing the Peloponnesian War, it comes after *Oedipus the King* in the chronology of the Oedipus story, and before *Antigone*. According to David Greene, who co-edited the University of Chicago series that now publishes Robert Fitzgerald's translation of the play—the one used in *The Gospel at Colonus*, currently being revived at the Lunt-Fontanne Theatre—*Antigone* was first produced around 441 B.C., *Oedipus the King* some fifteen years later, and *Oedipus at Colonus*, posthumously, in 404, the year after the destruction of the Athenian fleet at Aegospotami.

The action of the play revolves around an oracle's pronouncement that whatever city Oedipus chooses for his final resting place shall be blessed—divinely protected. When the play opens, news of this prophecy has got around, so that, after many years of wandering with only Antigone (and occasionally her sister, Ismene) to guide and comfort him, the old, blind beggar Oedipus, arriving at Colonus, outside Athens, finds himself suddenly very much sought after. Creon, the King of Thebes, wants him because the city is under attack by Polynices, Oedipus' son; Polynices needs him for victory in the coming battle with Eteocles, his brother.

There is no moral position stronger than to be suddenly wanted by those who have treated you badly, and the expression of righteous anger was Sophocles' forte. *Oedipus at Colonus* provides a real field day for moral-indignation buffs: it gives Oedipus a chance to vent his spleen on just about everyone who has ever given him a hard time—from an officious stranger to smug Creon, lording it over the House of Labdacus for all those years, and his own son Polynices, who, with his brother, had left reverence and filial piety to the girls. Oedipus tells them all exactly where they get off. The play is full of great speeches and confrontations, great rage and bitterness. . . .

SOUL STIRRERS AND ELECTRIC GUITARS

The production at the Lunt-Fontanne is essentially the same one that was seen by audiences at the Brooklyn Academy of Music in 1983 and was broadcast on PBS in 1985. Isabell Monk plays Antigone, as she did in the original production, and Morgan Freeman narrates the role of Oedipus, in the person of a Pentecostal preacher—for, as everyone will by now have heard, the show takes certain liberties with the play. Conceived and directed by Lee Breuer, with music by Bob Telson, *The Gospel at Colonus* is Sophocles' play recast as a black gospel service. Each of the roles is both spoken and sung, narrated and acted out—in most cases, by more than one person. Thus, Oedipus' part in the story is sometimes told by Mr. Freeman and sometimes sung by Clarence Fountain backed up by the Five Blind Boys of Alabama. Occasionally J.J. Farley and his blue-suited Soul Stirrers attend the five white-suited Blind Boys like a private chorus. Robert Earl Jones plays Creon wearing a mobster's white overcoat; Kevin Davis, full of sullen anger and bitterness, plays Polynices dressed largely in leather; the "Ode to Man" from *Antigone* is sung by the J.D. Steele Singers; Rev. Earl F. Miller performs the messenger speech like a call-and-response sermon; and Martin Jacox acts as Choragos, wailing on an electric guitar. Meanwhile, a full gospel choir, ebulliently [enthusiastically] led by J.D. Steele, and seated throughout on the scaffolding of Alison Yerxa's set, performs Mr. Telson's gospel settings for the choral odes, occasionally crying out responses as Mr. Freeman reads from what he calls "The Book of Oedipus."

A SONG WITH RHYTHMIC PACE

This song sung by the chorus in Oedipus at Colonus *has a rhythmic pace and simple yet powerful lyrics, both of which are hallmarks of gospel music.*

CHORUS:

Ah, God, to be where the pillagers make stand!
To hear the shout and brazen sound of war!
Or maybe on Apollo's sacred strand,
Or by that torchlit Eleusinian shore

Where pilgrims come, whose lips the golden key
Of sweet-voiced ministers has rendered still,
To cherish there with grave Persephonê
Consummate rest from death and mortal ill;

For even to those shades the warrior king
Will press the fighting on—until he take
The virgin sisters from the foemen's ring,
Within his country, for his country's sake!

The idea of superimposing Christian values on *Oedipus at Colonus* is both clever and problematic. Lee Breuer is not the first to notice the presence in the play of certain proto-Christian themes: sin and salvation, suffering and redemption, expiation [atonement for sin] and a spirit of divine grace that blows where it lists. Some of what is heard or seen toward the end of the play might even remind one of resurrection, rebirth, and life everlasting. Still, the only thing promised "for all time to come" is divine protection for Athens, and it is contingent on Oedipus' being dead: his bones have to be lying there in Athenian soil.

What happens at the end of *Oedipus at Colonus* and what sort of godhead, if any, Oedipus has been accorded are subjects of scholarly debate, but the Breuer version is unequivocal. At the end of the evening, Mr. Freeman, vocally accompanied by Mr. Fountain and the Five Blind Boys, and by much sobbing and lamentation, makes his way ceremoniously up a flight of stairs toward a doorway gleaming with dry-ice mystery and light. And when he does it's a dead cert that no one at the Lunt-Fontanne is thinking of the House of Labdacus.

GREAT POETRY BEAUTIFULLY RENDERED

The Gospel at Colonus is probably at its best on the symbolic level—where characters onstage become archetypal figures, embodying certain passions and predicaments. It's the level at which theatre becomes an occasion for hearing great poetry beautifully rendered. Listening to the rise and fall of Morgan Freeman's voice as he recites a choral ode, listening to Isabell Monk's cadences [vocal rhythms] and watching the shades of abstract virtues that cross her face—patience, devotion, generosity—you find yourself wondering what it would be like to see them perform Shakespeare, and, in wondering this, realize that a lack of music and oratory in the schooling of white American speech must account for half our inadequacy in performing the classics. The other half can be put down to the inability of so many Method actors to project anything other than feeling. Monk and Freeman know how to do more than emote, can actually hold an audience spellbound in the grip of someone else's words. The style of the production, too—mixing drama and narrative—is useful in suggesting, if not how tragedy was performed in the fifth century, at least something about how it may have been received. The chorus that spoke in the voice of one but had the body of many was there, after all, to get caught up in the drama *and* help tell the story. Even the device of having Oedipus played by seven men has the effect of emphasizing his magnitude and universality. And, of course, there's the music—more witty than stirring in the first half, and more stirring than funny in the second, though there's humor on both sides.

Where *The Gospel at Colonus* fails is at the axis at which theatre is supposed to make us care about the commerce between specific individuals. *Oedipus at Colonus* presents a great cast of characters, all of whom have a good deal to say (most of it of a very complex nature) about the fate of Oedipus. The text presented at the Lunt-Fontanne is cut to shreds: it's *Oedipus at Colonus* with most of the dialogue left out, lines, odes, and speeches reassigned and transposed—sometimes from other plays—and only enough bits of the long speeches left in for the story to hold its shape. Not once in the course of the evening are we stirred by a confrontation: at times, the figures that pace the stage might be almost anyone.

MOVING US TO STOMP AND CLAP

Lee Breuer's version of *Oedipus at Colonus* conveys neither the moral issues at stake in the situation that the play proposes nor anything of its drama. But so what? *The Gospel at Colonus* isn't about theatre or the values of fifth-century Athens; it's about American values—specifically, black culture and black music. Moreover, there is a sense in which Sophocles' play isn't really about Oedipus, either, a point at which its hero stops being simply Oedipus and becomes Athens at the end of the Peloponnesian War: like Oedipus, tired and beleaguered, ragged and set upon from all sides, an unwilling suppliant of her moral inferiors. To Athenians watching the play in the twilight of the Periclean era, Oedipus the achiever, the self-made king and solver of incomprehensible riddles, must have represented all the Athenian virtues. Just as it is possible for a contemporary audience to feel touched by Oedipus, if not for his own sake, then for that of the ghost of Athens, it ought to be possible for a purist to be moved by *The Gospel at Colonus.* The tradition of gospel music and the values it upholds—the importance of church and family—are as threatened today as war-torn Athens was. Athens held out until the very last moment: even after that decisive naval disaster, she endured siege and famine, fighting on like one of Sophocles' stubborn heroes, and didn't surrender until 404, the year after Sophocles died. In equating blind Oedipus with the black musician trying to make his way in a predominantly white world, in moving us all to stomp and clap, *The Gospel at Colonus* may not promote an understanding of Sophocles but it keeps faith in spirit with the culture that produced him.

An Opera Version of *Oedipus the King*

Arthur Holmberg

In the mid-1920s, the great Russian composer Igor Stravinsky (1882–1971) wrote an opera based on Sophocles' *Oedipus the King*, which had long been one of the composer's favorite plays. Stravinsky opted, as many modern scholars did (and still do), to use the term *Tyrannus* rather than *King* in the title, in order to convey more precisely the concept of tyranny that so disturbed the ancient Athenians who witnessed the first productions of the play. In this article, music commentator Arthur Holmberg explains how, in writing the music and adapting the play's text, the composer tried to express some of the original work's most basic underlying themes, especially the lead character's burning quest to discover his real identity.

Freud trivialized Oedipus. By focusing so narrowly on domestic melodrama, he overlooked the meaning and mystery of myth. Stravinsky's opera-oratorio comes much closer to catching the brooding exaltation, the pity and terror that activate the original.

Sophocles' tragedy is the most famous play in world literature. In the *Poetics*, Aristotle cites it as the supreme example of tragedy and uses it to prove the superiority of drama over other literary genres. . . . Sophocles' play remains not only the drama of dramas but arguably the greatest single work of the Western literary tradition.

It has become customary to refer to the play as *Oedipus Tyrannus*, a more exact title that indicates the play's political concerns—an indirect apologia for Athenian democracy that dramatizes the danger of placing too much power in the hands of any one man, since all human beings are fallible and vulnerable. The health of the *polis* [city-state] depends

From Arthur Holmberg, "Too Deep for Tears," *Opera News*, February 18, 1984. Reprinted by permission.

on a distribution of power and a careful system of checks and balances. The word *king* does not convey the negative connotations and fear of autocratic rule that the word *tyrannos* held for the Athenians. Modern readers tend to concentrate on Oedipus' personal struggle and overlook the work's social implications, but the tragedy is not only Oedipus', it is also Thebes'. Some scholars point to Pericles and Aspasia [the great Athenian statesman and his mistress] as the prototypes of Oedipus and Jocasta and see the play as a warning to Athens, which had itself undergone the terrors of a plague and would soon suffer defeat at the hands of Sparta after nearly a century of unrivaled political, economic and cultural preeminence. No less than individuals, powers and principalities, empires and dominions can also bring about their nemesis through *hybris*, the pride that goes before a fall.

GUILT AND PRIMAL TABOOS

Like all complex works of the imagination, Sophocles' play is open to various and contradictory interpretations. In the main, critics have approached it from three different perspectives. The most traditional interpret it as a drama of guilt and expiation. The play, they argue, was presented at a religious festival for Dionysus and was written to prove that men must walk in fear and reverence before the gods. Oedipus errs through tragic flaws—temper and intellectual pride—and thereby deserves his punishment. Ironically, the very qualities that brought him to rise bring him to fall; the gods grind slowly, but they grind fine. Morally as well as physically, we live in a cause-and-effect world governed by *logos*, an underlying world order. Humans, through freely willed acts, violate the fundamental principle of justice and only through a violent recoil can harmony and balance be restored. Oedipus' fall is a moral failure.

Opponents of this interpretation see Oedipus not as a victim of his own nature but of fate. Apollo, not Oedipus' flaws, is the antagonist. These critics contend that the Victorian notion of a tragic flaw came from misreading Aristotle. The word he uses, *hamartia*, means an error of judgment, or "missing the mark." It does not refer to an inherent character trait. Nothing Oedipus does merits such punishment—a catastrophe that encircles not only Oedipus but Jocasta, their guiltless children and the people of Thebes.

In Aeschylus' version, the sins of Laius bring down a

curse that destroys his house, but Sophocles' reduces human guilt. The oracles did not alert Laius until after Jocasta had conceived, and Sophocles has Oedipus kill Laius in legitimate self-defense. Moreover, his anger at Tiresias, while somewhat ill-considered, can be explained by his concern for the welfare of Thebes. Tiresias withholds information that would lead to the city's salvation. As for his pride, Oedipus behaves no differently from other epic heroes, who unabashedly vaunt their virtues. In addition, he is pious. He flees Corinth to avoid sin, and he sends Creon to Delphi to consult the oracle. His subjects love him; Oedipus is a kind and just ruler, a good man brought low by the inexplicable blows of fate. The final choral ode takes Oedipus as representative man and reminds the audience that human happiness is fragile: the days of one's glory are, by the laws of Apollo, the god of life, numbered. Tragedy can strike at any moment, and no one can escape his portion of sorrow. Oedipus' fall is an awareness that the gods are not with him. . . .

Also inscribed in the play is the conflict between primal taboo—which when violated disrupts the cosmos, results in physical pollution and demands violent retribution and ritual purification—and a more enlightened ethical and legal code which takes into account motive and intent. According to primitive belief, Oedipus is guilty. He killed his father and married his mother, the two most heinous crimes. The plague is a physical manifestation of this pollution. Blood guilt must be purged with blood. According to the more advanced concepts of Athenian jurisprudence, however, Oedipus, acting in ignorance and self-defense, is morally innocent.

EXPLAINING THE MYSTERY OF EVIL

All three of these major approaches to the play converge on the basic problem of all religion—how to explain the mystery of evil—and the basic problem of all philosophy: is man free? If we are not free, to what extent can we be held accountable for our acts? If Apollo, symbol of life, lays a snare for Oedipus at his birth, who bears the guilt, and what does this imply about the nature of the god and his laws? The vocabulary of the debate changes from age to age and from discipline to discipline—free will, grace, predestination, the elect, heredity, environment, determinism, sociobiology—but the question remains, and nowhere has it been posed with such power and vision as in Sophocles.

In 1925, when Igor Stravinsky felt the need to compose a large-scale dramatic work, he turned to *Oedipus Tyrannus*, the play he had loved most in his youth. The decision to recast the Greek into Latin needs some clarification. If, as Stravinsky maintains, he wanted a language the audience did not understand, coupled with the dignity of antiquity, why not retain the original Greek? Even more than Latin, it would have fulfilled the composer's search for a "pur langage sans office"—a language freed from the humdrum task of representing reality. "When I work with words in music," noted Stravinsky, "my musical appetite is set in motion by the sounds and rhythms of the syllables." What he sought, therefore, was language as signifier rather than signified—language reduced to the colors of its sounds. . . .

In the beginning, words and magic were one. In order to control the visible and invisible powers that govern life, to insure rain in due season, cure disease and propitiate the wrathful gods, shaman and priest chanted formulas understood by no one except the initiated. In this sense, ancient Greek would have served Stravinsky's purpose of making words incantation and opera rite. If Stravinsky opted for Latin, it was because he anticipated that any person in the audience with a Catholic or classical education (the work had its premiere in Paris) would have enough familiarity to catch the meaning of repeated words and phrases. Thus the composer could create a complex verbal and musical texture in which language wavers between intelligible discourse and magic formula. Also, the use of motifs from the Catholic liturgy—"gloria," "deus dixit," "lux facta est"—enhanced the aura. The word *oratorio* comes from the Latin verb "to pray.". . .

"A medium," Stravinsky explains, "not dead, but turned to stone and so monumentalized as to have become immune from all risk of vulgarization." The sensuous sounds of words interpenetrate the rhythms and colors of the music to form a sum greater than either part, a total sonic environment. "No translation of this passage," he observed . . . "can translate what I have done musically with the language. But there are many such [translations] . . . of my Russian vocal music. I am so disturbed by them [that] I prefer to hear those pieces in Russian or not at all. Fortunately, Latin is still permitted to cross borders—at least no one has yet proposed to translate my *Oedipus*, my *Psalms*, my *Canticum* and my *Mass*."

A Search for Self

In his opera-oratorio Stravinsky re-creates Sophocles' tragedy from the spirit of our times. The thrust of twentieth-century criticism is to see Oedipus as an existential allegory. His search for the criminal becomes a search for self. Oedipus, who guessed that the answer to the Sphinx's riddle was man, now has to answer the greater riddle: what manner of man am I? The detective story to find the killer of a king becomes a psychological and metaphysical quest. What the twentieth century most admires in Oedipus is his intellectual courage. When Tiresias and Jocasta warn him not to continue, he presses forward. "Skiam!" he shouts—I must know *who* I am, *what* my origin is. From the moment he knows *who* he is, he also knows *what* he is, and his tragedy begins.... The universe may not respond to the human need for radiance, clarity and unity, but Oedipus, alone and exiled, finds in himself the endurance to prevail. The Sphinx's riddle ("What walks on four legs in the morn, on two legs at noon and three legs at dusk?") becomes a prophecy that Oedipus himself fulfills, a banished blind man groping with a stick.

In many ways, the cultural and spiritual crisis in Europe when Stravinsky set about writing *Oedipus Rex* paralleled the upheavals in fifth-century Athens. World War I smashed empires, dynasties and Europe's confidence in itself.... The old gods—patriotism, culture, religion—had failed. Even science, which promised unlimited progress, became an avenging angel. Mustard gas, Big Berthas, Dreadnoughts, Zeppelins, submarines—the new technology brought curses as well as blessings, destruction, not salvation. Where among the fallen idols could one find a principle of belief? The sea of faith became a darkling plain.

Doubt and Self-Doubt

Athens too, when Sophocles wrote *Oedipus Tyrannus,* was passing through a moment of doubt and self-doubt. From acting as savior of Greece against the hordes of Persia she had turned to imposing an empire on the other Greek cities, which rapidly crumbled. Advances in philosophy, history, experimental science, medicine, mathematics and jurisprudence led many to question the Olympian gods as an adequate way of explaining the universe. "Man," declared Protagoras, "is the measure of all things." Let us use human

reason, not the old myths, to try to make sense of the world
and our lives.

What is man? What is his place in the universe, viewed
from a human perspective? The old answers no longer
seemed adequate, but reason could and would solve the riddles, problems, mysteries. Hippocrates started to diagnose
diseases by distinguishing one syndrome from another. Scientists devised a new physics based on atoms and pro-
pounded a theory of evolution which traced man's origin to
ocean slime. Gorgias and Hippias astounded the age with a
new mathematics. (The importance of numbers is under-
scored by many motifs in the drama, including *trivium*, the
meeting of three roads.) Socrates, who urged that "The un-
examined life is not worth living," inspired his students, including Plato, to ask questions. (*Oedipus Tyrannus* is a series
of questions.)...

It was a cultural revolution the likes of which the world
has never seen again. Though it laid the basis for all humanistic inquiry afterward, it was an age of anxiety. If the
old gods do not exist, who or what rules the universe? "A
whirlwind cast Zeus out and now reigns supreme," ex-
claims Pheidippides in Aristophanes' *The Clouds*.

The intellectual doubts of this age come to a head in Jocasta, whom literary critics, focusing on Oedipus, overlook.
From many points of view, she is the most interesting character in the play, and Stravinsky gave her the most sensuous,
seductive music. Many had come to distrust Delphi [location
of the famous oracle]—after all, it had favored Persia over
Greece, Sparta over Athens. It was unreliable, and forged oracles circulated. In the play, which turns on oracles, Jocasta
begins by questioning the god's priests. She ends by questioning the god himself. "As for prophecy," Sophocles' heroine de-
clares, "I would not look right or left because of it. . . . Chance
rules life." In one of his brightest moments, Stravinsky set to
music "Oracula, oracula, mentita sunt oracula," its obsessive
rhythms lingering long in memory.

Too Deep for Tears

Later in the play, Jocasta burns incense to the Lycean Apollo,
which may seem contradictory, but the gods and her relationship to them do not motivate Jocasta. What is important
to her are human relationships, the welfare of those she
loves. Sophocles pits her as a telling foil against Oedipus.

She can live with the frightening possibility that chance and a whirlwind rule the universe, but she cannot live if her human relationships are destroyed.

What Aristotle particularly admired was Sophocles' ability to bring together a reversal (*peripeteia*) and a recognition (*anagnorisis*). The *anagnorisis* is Oedipus' recognition of

---

OEDIPUS'S PROMISE

Oedipus promises his Theban subjects that he will find Laius's murderer in this excerpt from Knox's translation of Oedipus the King.

OEDIPUS

I shall make a proclamation, speaking as one who has no connection with this affair, nor with the murder. . . . I now proclaim to all of you, citizens of Thebes: whoever among you knows by whose hand Laius son of Labdacus was killed, I order him to reveal the whole truth to me.

If he is afraid to speak up, I order him to speak even against himself, and so escape the indictment, for he will suffer no unpleasant consequence except exile; he can leave Thebes unharmed. . . .

But if you keep silent—if someone among you refuses my offer, shielding some relative or friend, or himself—now, listen to what I intend to do in that case. That man, whoever he may be, I banish from this land where I sit on the throne and hold the power; no one shall take him in or speak to him. He is forbidden communion in prayers or offerings to the gods, or in holy water. Everyone is to expel him from their homes as if he were himself the source of infection which Apollo's oracle has just made known to me. That is how I fulfill my obligations as an ally to the god and to the murdered man. As for the murderer himself, I call down a curse on him, whether that unknown figure be one man or one among many. May he drag out an evil death-in-life in misery. And further, I pronounce a curse on myself if the murderer should, with my knowledge, share my house; in that case may I be subject to all the curses I have just called down on these people here. . . .

On those who do not co-operate with these measures I call down this curse in the gods' name: let no crop grow out of the earth for them, their wives bear no children. Rather let them be destroyed by the present plague, or something even worse. But to you people of Thebes who approve of my action I say this: May justice be our ally and all the gods be with us forever!

who he is and the limits of man's existence. The *peripeteia* is twofold, the reversal in his fortune from a position of honor and power to one of shame and exile, as well as the fact that everything he has done brings about the opposite of what he expected. Almost every speech in the play contains an astounding instance of dramatic irony. Oedipus promises his subjects he will find the murderer and save the city. He does, little realizing he himself is the murderer. Jocasta seeks to soothe her husband's troubled spirit by proving that oracles lie, yet the word she uses to calm him, *trivium*, stokes his fear. And Tiresias, who is blind, sees more clearly than Oedipus, who takes pride in his intellect.

Only through great suffering, and after he has lost his physical sight, does Oedipus attain Tiresias' level of wisdom. Sophocles exploits dramatic irony to dramatize how human beings who trust their eyes and minds fall prey to delusions. Our real situation is far different from what we imagine, and we cannot grasp this until we see with our hearts.

Stravinsky's music—objective, cool, acerbic [bitter]—was the perfect medium to translate the irony and anxiety of fifth-century Athens into the irony and despair of twentieth-century Europe. Dissonance, tonal ambiguity, polytonality [various musical devices]—all resolve into beautifully familiar chords. "How happy I was when I discovered that chord!" Stravinsky exulted over the D-major triad that ends Oedipus' "Lux facta est." Throughout, hypnotic rhythms borrowed from Beethoven's Fifth Symphony capture Sophocles' sense of fate.

What, finally, are we to make of a Greek tragedy sung in Church Latin in an eclectic musical idiom that parodies the history of Western music? The score reverberates with distorted echoes of Bach, Handel, Gluck, Rameau, Mozart, Beethoven, Verdi, Mussorgsky, Russian folk tunes and liturgical music. Ritual and art, art and ritual...these are Stravinsky's fragments shored against the ruin.

Now, 2,400 years after its premiere, *Oedipus Tyrannus* continues to stir because it defines the human condition with clarity and compassion, dramatizing emotions and thoughts that lie too deep for tears. Thanks to Stravinsky, Sophocles' hero speaks to us in a distinctively modern voice. Tragedy is not dead, and will not die, as long as Stravinsky's Oedipus continues to sing.

Sophocles on Film

Jon Solomon

It was perhaps inevitable that the modern medium
of film, always searching for great stories to tell,
would turn to the classic dramas of the ancient
Greeks, including those of Sophocles. Not surprisingly, filmmakers have attempted to adapt *Oedipus
the King* for the screen more than any other ancient
play. Unfortunately though, as classical scholar and
film critic Jon Solomon comments in his book *The
Ancient World in the Cinema,* the results of these efforts to film Sophocles and his contemporaries have
not often been successful. The reasons that many
filmmakers have missed the mark vary considerably,
Solomon argues. On the one hand, they sometimes
try too hard to adhere to the original stage conventions Sophocles used. On the other, they often fail to
include important ancient conventions that would
enliven the onscreen action. The net result of both of
these ill-conceived approaches is usually cinematic
boredom. Nevertheless, Solomon says, a few film
versions of Sophocles are worth the effort to track
down and watch.

There were hundreds of tragedies produced in Athens in the
fifth century B.C., but only thirty-three survive reasonably
intact. Of these thirty-three extant Greek tragedies, six have
been turned into feature films: Sophocles' *Antigone* and
Oedipus Rex, and Euripides' *Bacchae, Electra, Medea,* and
Trojan Women. Despite the high attrition rate, it is no small
achievement for a play to be "running" on the silver screen
some two thousand four hundred years after its Athenian
debut at the Dionysian Festival.

Oedipus Rex, the well-known Sophoclean drama about
the king who has unknowingly killed his father and married
his mother, has been made into five different films ranging

From Jon Solomon, *The Ancient World in the Cinema* (New York: A.S. Barnes, 1978).
Reprinted by permission of the author.

from Giuseppe De Liguoro's *Edipo Re* (1910) to Philip Saville's *Oedipus the King* (1967). Tyrone Guthrie's 1957 version
was performed by the Stratford Shakespearean Festival Players of Canada. A very learned film in that all the players
wear masks and recite their Sophoclean lines from William
Butler Yeats's translation, *King Oedipus* fails to better itself
through the film medium. There is only one set; there is no
action; there are no quick or graceful movements; and there
is no photographic enhancement. To shoot a closeup of a
man in a mask is only to shoot a closeup of the mask; the facial expressions do not change, and so the effect of the shot
will hardly change. The masks themselves are rather fetch-
ing, brazen images of haggard cheeks and troubled brows,
but they alone cannot carry the effect of the drama.

TENSIONS AND TWISTED IRONIES

King Oedipus does not disappoint its audience in terms of its
drama. The fantastic intricacies and twists of Sophocles' plot
have earned *Oedipus Rex* the reputation of being one of the
greatest plays ever written. Any literary, theatrical, or cinematic audience devours the hidden ironies and cruelties of
the Theban king's fate: when Oedipus thinks he is free of his
fate because his supposed "father" Polybus has died of natural causes; or when Jocasta tries to relieve her father-
murdering husband (and son), telling him that not he but a
"brigand" slew her first husband Laius "at the crossroads";
or when Oedipus realizes then that he himself might possibly be the murderer; or when the blind seer Teiresias warns
Oedipus that "he sees but does not see," and then this results
in Oedipus' blinding himself; or when Oedipus tells Jocasta
that he is not afraid to find out that he might be born of slave
origins while the audience knows that he will find out much
worse. No film can ruin the story, its Sophoclean ironies,
and its powerful impact. But a film has the responsibility of
being a film and should in some way look like cinema and
not like a mere play on film. This *King Oedipus* fails to do.
Even if *King Oedipus'* archaistic [primitive-looking] style is
close to the ancient Greek dramatic style, still, a film has a
responsibility to filmdom.

1967 saw two very different film versions of *Oedipus Rex*.
The first was a Pier Paolo Pasolini voyage into, to use Pasolini's own word, "meta-history." The modern prologue and
epilogue delved into Pasolini's own Freudian interpretation

of the Oedipus complex; he emphasizes the father's resentment toward the son much more than the son's textbook resentment toward the father. Though the Sophoclean drama is stretched irretrievably, many critics, including Pasolini himself, have considered the modern prologue one of his best sequences.

The "ancient" part of the drama is based on Pasolini's own translation of both *Oedipus Rex* and *Oedipus at Colonus*. Shot in Morocco and set to Romanian and Japanese ethnomusics, these "ancient" sequences reenact only selected Sophoclean scenes, and they are embellished by several mythologically oriented scenes such as Oedipus' visit to the oracle of Delphi and his brief verbal battle with the Sphinx. . . .

Drawing fine acting and a thorough intensity out of his cast, Victor Saville outdid by far *The Silver Chalice* [his earlier film, which received poor critical reviews] with his 1967 version of *Oedipus the King*. It boasted an arrogant, strong-willed Oedipus (Christopher Plummer), a matronly, lovely Jocasta (Lilli Palmer), a capable, kingly Creon (Richard Johnson), and a weighty, profound, and imposingly prophetic Teiresias (Orson Welles). The film was shot along the angular, chipped limestone *cavea* of the ancient Greek theater at Dodona, and this setting amidst the ruins helped to equate Oedipus' crumbling claims to normalcy with the visual surroundings. Welles's Teiresias looms large over Oedipus and the Theban elders with his divine admonitions and human anger, like lofty Mt. Pelion over the spreading Aegean Sea. The tensions and twisted ironies of Sophocles' poetry are ever present, and even the relatively unpoetic shepherd and messenger speeches breathe with life and absorbing narrative. Saville shows the horrors of Jocasta's hanging and Oedipus' blinding with just enough realism; they suggest the extreme horror to which Oedipus' stubborn search for his origins inevitably lead, yet the blood is not excessive; Oedipus' overlooking of the truth about his birth can end only in blinding the same eyes that "saw but did not see." Lastly, the film's shots of the scrubby northern Greek scenery, of the curvilinear [curved] patterns of the Dodona theater, and of the psychological flashbacks in Oedipus' mind—that day at the crossroads where he "killed a man"—create a depth and scope at which no stage production could possibly aim.

MISSING THE SONG AND DANCE

Despite the merits of [Saville's film of] *Oedipus the King* it would never have won first prize at an ancient Athenian contest. It would have pleased the judges (and Aristotle) with its plot, its characters, poetry, and philosophy, but it lacks the spectacle and music that changed, at some stubbornly obscure point in Athenian history, mere poetic dialogue into full-blown theater. In essence, the problem is the same one film directors meet in portraying a cinematic Christ: too much cinematically uncreative reverence produces boredom, whether this reverence is directed toward the Christ or toward the Greek dramatic chorus. Modern film directors generally treat the Greek chorus with too much respect, but this type of unwarranted stiffness and unauthentic purity destroys the chorus' original effect. *Oedipus the King* presents the chorus as a group of robed and bearded elders; fine. They interpret, digest, and react to the drama unfolding around them; fine. But they merely recite their lyrics in unison, individually, or in sequence, and they never dance a step. This is where the film lacks its authentic music and spectacle. Ancient Athenian tragedy, for all its psychological and theological profundity, for all its macabre plots and immortal poetry, appeared on the ancient stage with a full battery of ancient music and "special effects." To omit the musical spectacle is the same as if someone were to find the script for Fred Astaire's *Top Hat* two thousand years from now, refilm the script while omitting the dances, and merely recite the lyrics to "The Piccolino" and "I'm Putting on My Top Hat." A chorus by nature and definition, whether it be an ancient Greek chorus or a Busby Berkeley or Hermes Pan [modern stage and film choreographers] chorus, sings and dances. Without song and dance, be it ever so archaic or limited in its production, a Greek tragedy can be only a skeleton of its real self.

Other than the simplistically reduced dramatization of *Oedipus at Colonus* in *Hercules Unchained,* no other major film has recorded a Sophoclean play with the exception of *Antigone* (1961). Despite a noble attempt by Irene Papas in the title role, the film does not really offer an invigorated interpretation of this ancient drama based on the conflict between human law and divine law. The acting is for the most part as monolithic [rigid] and austere as the setting, and so when Creon weeps, realizing that his insistence on human law and order has resulted in the deaths of his wife and son, it means little emotionally to the viewer. This film about Oedipus' daughter (and sister) also suffers from lack of respect for the film medium. Only one exterior shot is used very effectively: the deeply shadowed cave in which Antigone and Haemon die is viewed from the inside out; this subjective shot contrasts strongly the gloom in which the deaths must occur and the Hellenic brightness outside. Otherwise, the visual elements in this all-Greek production are disappointing, though the English subtitles—the soundtrack is in modern Greek—could not be avoided. *Antigone* would work well for classroom instruction, but as artistic cinema it is mediocre.

Oedipus at Colonus Is a Statement of Hope

Robert Fitzgerald

In *Oedipus the King*, Sophocles brought the character of Oedipus toppling down from the heights of kingly grace to the depths of despair, blindness, and poverty. This punishment, as Athenian audiences well knew, was the will of the gods, for Oedipus had committed some of the most terrible sins possible. But the gods were not totally merciless, as the playwright demonstrated when he brought Oedipus back to the stage one last time in the final play of his long career—*Oedipus at Colonus*. In this commentary on the play (accompanying his well-known translation of the entire Oedipus cycle), scholar Robert Fitzgerald explains how the fallen Oedipus, in becoming the instrument of a new round of god-sent justice, atones for his former sins and redeems himself, finally making a mysterious, apparently supernatural physical and moral transition from disgrace back to grace. This marked Sophocles' final word as a tragedian, for he died soon after writing it. In effect then, he left to posterity a statement of hope, the assurance that no matter how far humanity might sink, it would always be, in God's eyes, worthy of redemption.

Oedipus at Colonus is reckoned on ancient authority to have been the last of more than one hundred plays by its author. It was composed probably in 406 B.C., when Sophocles was eighty-nine years old. Some of the play's peculiar interest lies in this fact, and in various matters implied by this fact. At the time of its composition the Peloponnesian War between Athens and Sparta had been in progress for more than a quarter of a century. To Colonus, where he was born, and to the great and hard-pressed city of which he was a beloved

Excerpted from "Oedipus at Colonus," in *Sophocles, the Oedipus Cycle: An English Version*, translated by Dudley Fitts and Robert Fitzgerald. Copyright ©1941 by Harcourt Brace & Company; renewed 1969 by Robert Fitzgerald. Reprinted by permission of the publisher.

citizen, Sophocles paid his tribute in this play. Though Athens was still undefeated her lands had already been laid waste, and the verses about the olive trees may well have moved their first readers or auditors to tears. The play was not produced in the theater until 401 B.C., four years after the death of Sophocles and three years after the starvation and capitulation of Athens. *Oedipus at Colonus* is therefore one of the last considerable works known to us from the period of Athenian genius.

Like the six other extant [surviving] plays of Sophocles, it is the work of a mind in the highest degree orderly, penetrating and sensitive, an enlightened mind aware of the moral issues in human action, and a reverent mind aware of the powers that operate through time and fortune on human affairs. But it is first of all the work of an artist, a maker of plots and poetry, and it is only from the ever-ambiguous expression of art that we may divine his thought or his theme. Accordingly we have here no such lucid a revelation of Athenian intellect as we find in the history of Thucydides or the dialogues of Plato. For its original audience the play shimmered with implications that are lost to us. Yet even we cannot fail to see in it the last, long reach toward truth of an artist who was formed by his great epoch [era] and who perfectly represents it.

A Thirst for Blood

It would be hard to imagine any tribulation more severe than that endured by Oedipus, king of Thebes. At the summit of his power he discovered himself damned, by his own pertinacity [stubborn persistence] discovered that he had horribly offended against the decencies by which men must live. In one day he fell from sovereignty and fame to self-blinded degradation, and later he was driven into exile. He comes on the stage a blind beggar led by a girl. The Athenians had no romantic notions about vagabondage or exile; in their eyes Oedipus had been reduced to the worst extremity, barring slavery, that a noble man could suffer.

But the atmosphere of the place to which the old man comes is an atmosphere of shadiness, blessedness and peace; and the contrast between Oedipus in his rags and the beauty of Colonus is an effect of which we are at once aware, an effect not unlike that of Odysseus' awakening in the pretty island of Phaeacia [an episode in Homer's *Odyssey*].

Only here the poet's purposes are not so simple. For this is a grove sacred to the Furies, and the Furies are those spirits of retribution by whom sinners, murderers especially, and Oedipus in particular, have been pursued. It is furthermore well known to Sophocles' audience that in the *Eumenides* of Aeschylus, years before, these spirits were persuaded by Athena to reconcile themselves to the superior rule of Athenian law. Thus gentled, so to speak, in Attica, they have nevertheless great intrinsic power, and must be treated with tact. And they are indeed, as we see here symbolized, the divinities with whom Oedipus must make his peace.

To the sentimentalist there may be something odd in the character and demeanor of this old man whom adversity

---

OEDIPUS'S MYSTERIOUS DISAPPEARANCE

In this scene from Fitzgerald's translation of Sophocles' final play, Oedipus at Colonus, *a messenger tells how he saw the once miserable Oedipus mysteriously disappear, apparently taken into the embrace of the gods who have at last forgiven him.*

MESSENGER:
    Citizens, the briefest way to tell you
    Would be to say that Oedipus is no more;
    But what has happened cannot be told so simply—
    It was no simple thing. . . .

    You know, for you were witnesses, how he
    Left this place with no friend leading him,
    Acting, himself, as guide for all of us.
    Well, when he came to the steep place in the road,
    The embankment there, secured with steps of brass,
    He stopped in one of the many branching paths. . . .

    He sat down and undid his filthy garments;
    Then he called his daughters and commanded
    That they should bring him water from a fountain
    For bathing and libation to the dead. . . .
    [They] soon came back with water for their father;
    Then helped him properly to bathe and dress.

    When everything was finished to his pleasure . . .
    He put his arms around them, and said to them:

    "Children, this day your father is gone from you.
    All that was mine is gone. You shall no longer
    Bear the burden of taking care of me—
    I know it was hard, my children.—And yet one word

might properly have purged into sweetness and resignation. His fund of both these qualities is limited. The dignity of Oedipus is never in doubt, but observe that this dignity is not of the sort associated with patriarchs. It is not incompatible with a scornful and artful wit, nor with a sort of fighting alertness: witness his persuasive remarks to the Attic elders who try to dismiss him from the grove. Nor is it incompatible with a definite savagery. The quick anger in which he killed his father and goaded Teiresias, long ago, into telling him the truth—it is, if anything, fiercer in his old age. A literal thirst for blood appears in his prophecy to Theseus of war between Thebes and Athens, and this primitivism in Oedipus is all the more evident by contrast with the calm

Frees us of all the weight and pain of life:
That word is love. . . .

Children, you must show your nobility,
And have the courage now to leave this spot.
You must not wish to see what is forbidden,
Or hear what may not afterward be told.
But go—go quickly. Only the lord Theseus [the king]
May stay to see the thing that now begins."

This much every one of us heard him say,
And then we came away with the sobbing girls.
But after a little while as we withdrew
We turned around—and nowhere saw that man,
But only the king, his hands before his face,
Shading his eyes as if from something fearful,
Awesome and unendurable to see.
Then very quickly we saw him do reverence
To Earth and to the powers of the air,
With one address to both.

                But in what manner
Oedipus perished, no one of mortal men
Could tell but Theseus. It was not lightning,
Bearing its fire from Zeus, that took him off;
No hurricane was blowing.
But some attendant from the train of Heaven
Came for him; or else the underworld
Opened in love the unlit door of earth.
For he was taken without lamentation,
Illness or suffering; indeed his end
Was wonderful if mortal's ever was.

Athenian hero. Against Creon and against his son he becomes a tower of passion and disgust.

OEDIPUS ATONES FOR HIS SINS

In what, then, is his dignity? Why is he not merely an obsessed and vindictive old man? It should be remembered
that one of Oedipus' distinguishing qualities was, in the first
place, his intelligence. He saved Thebes once by solving the
riddle of the Sphinx. He saved the city again by solving with
furious persistence the riddle of his own birth. And in this
play we see once more the working of that intellect, driving
this time toward a transcendence [rise to supreme impor-
tance] of the purely human. During the years in which Oedipus has probed his own guilt he has come to terms with it.
Though innocent of willful murder or incest, he has made
expiation [atonement for sin] for what he recognized as his
share of responsibility in those acts. Without reference to
Freud we may perceive that in this whole fable of Oedipus
the great poet is giving us to understand that the nature of
man is darker than men believe it to be. Yet Oedipus is not
penitent, for he has also recognized that the powers control-
ling life have, in a sense, chosen him as their example and
instrument.

Thus it is not alone through passive suffering that the
spirit of Oedipus attains power and blessedness. His rage
and sternness in his last hours are the means of an affirma-
tion, the most profound this poet could make. We recognize
Oedipus' right to pass sentence on Creon and on his son,
though by our first and easy standards neither would seem
to deserve the curse pronounced on him. Creon is tricky and
heartless, but he is "obeying the command of the State";
Polyneices has been thoughtless of his father and fiercely
jealous of his brother, but he does not seem a bad young
man. In the larger context of Oedipus' fate, however, we may
discern that their sins of meanness, of avarice, of irrever-
ence, are no less grave than the sins of passion for which
Oedipus was punished: that in condemning them to the
merciless justice soon to descend, Oedipus acts thoroughly
in accord with a moral order which his own experience has
enabled him to understand.

And this may clarify for us the beautiful ending of the
play. Oedipus has indeed endured his suffering with
courage, but it is not until he has acted, and acted as the

agent of divine justice, that the passionate man is fit to embody and to symbolize human divinity. Only then the Furies stand at his side; only then the gods receive him. And only then is bitterness lifted from him. His farewell to his daughters is the final word of Oedipus and of the tragedian. For, as a great Polish writer has written, "suffering is the lot of man, but not inevitable failure or worthless despair which is without end—suffering, the mark of manhood, which bears within its pain a hope of felicity like a jewel set in iron."

APPENDIX A

THE ORIGINS OF THEATER

The theater as people know it today—actors playing roles before an audience of spectators—was born in ancient Greece. Of that much scholars are sure. However, the exact origins of various theatrical conventions, or basic elements and practices, such as comedy, tragedy, and acting, remain shrouded in mystery. The Greeks, Egyptians, and other ancient peoples left very few written descriptions of themselves and their lives before the sixth century B.C. And of the primitive peoples that preceded them, all that we know is what scientists can deduce from studying bones, crude tools, and other decaying artifacts. So it is not surprising that frustrated scholars find the development of drama difficult to trace. "It is exasperating that the origin of something so significant should be so obscure," comments historian Lionel Casson. "No one knows for certain under what circumstances or precisely when the Greeks got the brilliant idea of having men impersonate imaginary characters."

STORIES TOLD THROUGH DANCE

Yet while the exact origins of drama may be obscure, it has been possible to make educated guesses about how people first began acting out certain events from their lives. Anthropologists (scientists who study human cultures) believe that early storytelling was one source of drama. According to this view, primitive hunters may have reenacted their hunting exploits for members of the family or tribe gathered around the campfire, as well as for their gods. In this context, the hunter would have taken on the role of actor and his listeners that of audience. Such early storytelling probably predated the development of complex language. So, anthropologists believe, initially it likely took the form of dance. As famed theatrical scholar Sheldon Cheney puts it:

> After the activities that secure to primitive peoples the material necessities, food and shelter, the dance comes first. It is the earliest outlet for emotion, and the beginning of the

arts. . . . Primitive man, poor in means of expression, with only the rudimentary beginnings of spoken language, universally expressed his deeper feelings through measured movement. . . . He danced for pleasure and as ritual. He spoke in dance to his gods, he prayed in dance and gave thanks in dance. By no means all this activity was dramatic or theatric; but in his designed movement was the germ of drama and of theater. . . . The noises man made, as he rhythmically moved, took on the measure of the swaying body and the tapping feet, gradually became war-song or prayer, developed into traditional tribal chant, [and] ultimately led to conscious poetry.

In most cultures the poetry of storytelling remained, for the most part, a part of religious ritual. Indeed, in Greece, as in other lands, formal dramatic poetry, along with music and dance, early became associated with religious ceremony. In particular, poetry was prominent in the rituals associated with the god Dionysus. In the early Greek myths, according to theater historian Oscar G. Brockett,

Dionysus was the son of Zeus (the greatest of Greek gods). . . . Reared by satyrs [mythical creatures, half-man and half-goat] he was killed, dismembered, and resurrected. As a god he was associated with fertility, wine, and revelry, while the events of his life linked him with . . . the cycle of the seasons, and the recurring pattern of birth, maturity, death, and rebirth. Through their rites, Dionysian worshippers sought a mystical union with the primal [most primitive] creative urge. On a more practical level, they sought to promote fertility: to guarantee the return of spring . . . and ample harvests.

THE GOAT-SONG

Worship of Dionysus, along with that of the other Greek gods, developed between the fourteenth and eighth centuries B.C. Little is known about this formative period of the people now referred to as the classical Greeks, whose splendid literature and art of the fifth and fourth centuries B.C. so influenced later civilizations, including today's. What is certain is that by the eighth century B.C. Dionysian ritual had developed a kind of poetry and ceremony known as dithyramb. This special form of verse, sung and danced to by the worshipers, became the highlight of the religious festivals dedicated to the god. The dithyramb, which told the story of Dionysus or in some way honored him, widened over time to include other gods, as well as some human heroes. The dithyramb also took on an increasingly dramatic form in which a priest led a group of worshipers, called a chorus, in chanting and dancing before the rest of the congregation. No examples of this verse have survived. But the opening of *The Suppliants*, a play by the fifth-century B.C. playwright Aeschylus [older books often use the spelling Aeschulus], probably captures the general form and atmosphere of the original dithyrambic procession. To the music of flutes and cymbals, a chorus of fifty maidens clad in white robes approaches an altar and rhythmically chants:

> Zeus! Lord and guard of suppliant hands!
> Look down benign [favorably] on us who crave
> Thine aid—whom winds and waters drave [drove]
> From where, through drifting shifting sands,
> Pours [the river] Nilus to the wave.

Certain men, at first probably priests, became adept at composing new versions of dithyramb. By creating material specifically to be performed before an audience, they may have been, in a sense, the first playwrights. This is certainly how Aristotle saw it. In his *Poetics*, written in the late fourth century B.C., he theorized that tragedy, the first definite form of drama, originated in Dionysian ritual. Tragedy, said Aristotle,

> certainly began in improvisations [spontaneous pieces] ... originating with the authors of the dithyramb ... which still survive ... in many of our cities. And its advance [as drama] after that was little by little, through their improving on whatever they had before them at each stage.

Supporters of this view point out that the dithyramb was also called "goat-song" because of the involvement of men dressed as satyrs in the ceremony. The term "tragedy," they say, probably developed from the Greek words *tragos*, meaning goat, and *odi*, meaning song.

THE SUSPENSE OF ANTICIPATION

Another source of drama in Greece was epic poetry. For centuries, wandering poets known as bards had recited the heroic deeds of gods and human heroes from Greece's dim past. Homer, a legendary bard possibly of the ninth century B.C., was credited with composing the two most famous epic poems, the *Iliad* and the *Odyssey*. The first told the tale of the Greeks' ten-year siege of the powerful kingdom of Troy to rescue Sparta's Queen Helen, who had been abducted by a Trojan prince. The other epic recounted the adventures of the Greek hero Odysseus (or Ulysses) on his way back from the siege.

At first, presentation of the epics was informal. A bard merely stood before a group of townspeople and recited the

stories. In time, however, as Greek society became more or-
ganized and urbanized, such reciting was more formal. In
the eighth and seventh centuries B.C., city-states became the
main focus of Greek civilization. Each of these tiny independent nations consisted of a central town and its surrounding
villages and farms. By the mid-sixth century, Athens, located
on the Attic peninsula in eastern Greece, had become the
largest and most influential of the city-states. It had also become the most cultured, with the government spending
growing sums to promote the arts and public festivals. In
about 566 B.C., seeking to enhance a popular festival, the
Athenian leader Solon instituted the *rhapsodia*, contests in
which various reciters delivered portions of the *Iliad* and
Odyssey before a large crowd.

These formal dramatic recitations, like the dithyramb, became very popular with the Athenian populace. Audiences
found both presentations exciting and moving, even though
they already knew the plots and outcomes. As theater
scholar Edmund Fuller explains:

> It is the peculiar power of drama that a play can be utterly
> gripping to its audience even when everyone knows perfectly
> well how it is going to end. Indeed, it often draws its greatest
> force from the fact that we *do* know what is coming. The sus-
> pense of anticipation is greater than that of surprise, for the
> real nature of suspense is anguish, concern for the characters
> because of our sympathy for them. What fascinates us is how
> they respond to what happens.

THE FIRST ACTOR

Later, around 534 B.C., Athens began holding a lavish annual
festival known as the City Dionysia, in honor of Dionysus.
Both formal dithyramb and *rhapsodia* were presented at this
festival, which featured Athens's most popular dramatic
contest yet. The first winner of this contest was a poet
named Thespis, who developed the dramatic presentations
into a new form called tragedy. This first version of what is
now recognized as a theatrical play utilized most of the elements of the dithyramb and the *rhapsodia*, but added some
important new ideas. Among the innovations of Thespis, for
instance, was the addition of a chorus to the *rhapsodia*. The
members of the chorus recited in unison some of the lines
and also commented on the events of the story, to focus audience attention more on the passion, plight, and suffering
of the heroes. Thespis's other novel idea was actually to im-

personate, rather than just tell about, the story's heroes. Theater historian Phyllis Hartnoll states:

> The great innovation that Thespis made was to detach himself from the chorus [of both dithyramb and *rhapsodia*] and, in the person of the god or hero whose deeds were celebrated, to engage in dialogue with it. He was thus the first actor as well as the first manager [producer-director]. The step he took was even more revolutionary than it seems to us, for he was the first unsanctified person [nonpriest] who dared to assume the character of a god.

In a sense, Thespis created the formal theater overnight. In utilizing dialogue between himself, the first actor, and the chorus, he introduced the basic convention of theatrical plays, namely, characters reciting set speeches, the content of which moves the story along. He also experimented with ways of disguising himself so that he could portray different characters in the same dramatic piece. He eventually decided on masks, which became another basic convention of Greek, and later Roman, theater. In addition, Thespis helped define the role of the audience. By enlarging the dithyramb into a piece of art and entertainment, he transformed the congregation into a true theater audience. For these innovations, Thespis became a theater immortal. As drama historian Marion Geisinger relates:

> The name of Thespis has come down to us in the use of the word *thespian* as a synonym for actor. Actually, the term seems originally to have referred to touring actors, because in ancient Greek vase paintings, Thespis is usually depicted seated on a cart; the tradition was that Thespis would take his actors [chorus members] around in this cart, which they used as a stage or performing platform. Whatever the reason, it seems most fitting to commemorate the first actor in the Western world by dubbing all those who have followed him with his name.

THE EARLY PLAYS

For subjects, Thespis and the playwrights who adopted his new form of entertainment and competed with him relied on the standard Greek myths, as well as on the tales in the *Iliad* and other epics now lost. They also depicted important recent historical events, especially attacks by the Persians on Greek cities in Asia Minor, what is now Turkey. Unfortunately, none of the plays of Thespis or his contemporaries have survived. Among these writer-actor-managers were Choerilus, who wrote some 160 plays and won the City

Dionysia contest thirteen times, and Pratinas, who supposedly wrote 18 tragedies. Phrynichus, another popular writer, first won the contest sometime around 510 B.C. His most famous play was *The Fall of Miletus*, about the Persian takeover of the most prosperous Greek city in Asia Minor. According to the Greek historian Herodotus, this play was so moving that the audience burst into tears and city officials fined Phrynichus one thousand drachmas, a large sum of money, for upsetting the citizenry.

Although the plays by Phrynichus, Choerilus, and Pratinas are lost, scattered fragments of these works and a few descriptions of them by later writers provide a rough idea of what the performances were like. Scholar James H. Butler, in *The Theater and Drama of Greece and Rome*, fills in some gaps:

> In performance, early Greek tragedies consisted of a series of acted episodes performed by one ... actor who also conversed with the leader of a chorus. During this action, chorus members reacted in patterned movements and gestures to what was happening.... Between episodes the chorus danced, recited in recitative [spoken words with musical accompaniment], and sang choral odes [songs] that related to past events or foreshadowed what was about to happen.

As such performances became increasingly elaborate and dramatic, the City Dionysia festival developed into a major holiday attraction, eagerly awaited each year by the populace. Covering several days at the end of March, the festival was open to all Greeks. The Athenian government wisely took the opportunity to use the celebration as a showcase of Athens's wealth and cultural achievements. To this end, the state financed the theater building and its maintenance, paid fees to the actors, and possibly the playwrights, and also provided prizes for the dramatic contests. All the other expenses of play production were the responsibility of the *choregi*, well-to-do Athenians asked by the state to help with the festival. These citizens were chosen by lot each year, and each *choregus* was assigned to a specific playwright. As Marion Geisinger explains:

> The *choregus* paid for the costumes, the sets, the training of the chorus, whatever supers (non-speaking extra roles) were required by the script, and the musicians. Obviously, the assignment of a generous *choregus* was an advantage to a playwright; that of a niggardly [cheap] one, a disadvantage.... Unhappy playwrights often felt that their failure to win the competition at the festival was the result of their being unable to mount their works properly, owing to the assignment of a stingy *choregus*.

The playwrights themselves also had weighty duties. In addition to writing plays, they acted in them, trained the chorus, composed the music, staged the dances, and supervised all other aspects of production. In fact, they were so involved in instructing others that at the time they were known as *didaskali*, or teachers.

OSCAR NIGHT IN ATHENS

The playwrights rehearsed their works for months, right up until the beginning of the festival. On the first day, they, their *choregi* and chorus members, along with important public officials, took part in a stately and majestic procession. This colorful parade wound its way through the city and ended at the Theater of Dionysus, at the foot of the Acropolis, the stony hill on which the city's main temples and public buildings rested. After the public sacrifice of a bull to Dionysus, the dramatic competitions began. First came the dithyrambic contests. Then, over the course of the next few days, each of three playwrights presented three tragedies. In the late sixth century B.C., tragedy was still the main dramatic form, as comedy was not yet well developed or popular. When comedies eventually began to be performed at the City Dionysia in 501 B.C., they took place at night, after day-long presentations of tragedy.

The most eagerly awaited moment of the festival was the awards ceremony, in many ways an ancient counterpart of today's Oscar night. Lionel Casson states:

> A panel of ten judges issued four lists containing, respectively, the order in which they rated the tragic playwrights, comic playwrights, tragic leading actors, and comic leading actors. The victors—and that meant those who topped the lists; only first place really counted—were crowned with ivy, and the *choregi* hurried off to arrange farewell banquets for their casts.

As popular and exciting as these early festivals were, they were merely a prelude to what was to come. In the fifth century B.C. Athens produced a brief but magnificent burst of cultural activity, the brilliant results of which would thrill and awe the world ever after. Among the city's artists were a handful of gifted playwrights, among them Aeschylus, Sophocles, Euripides, and Aristophanes, who would in a stroke create the model for great theater for all times.

APPENDIX B

GREEK THEATRICAL PRODUCTION

As their early theaters and dramatic presentations evolved, the Greeks developed most of the aspects and conventions of play production that became standard through the ages. Among these were the use of scenery, costumes and disguises, chorus, dancing, and music, as well as acting styles and special visual and sound effects. The Greeks also built the first permanent theaters, some of which are still in use. All the theaters in later Western societies, from Rome to the present day, have employed variations of the basic physical layout devised by the Greeks.

We will never know exactly how the Greeks used these theatrical conventions and how their plays appeared on stage. The last authentic Greek productions were presented more than two thousand years ago. And later cultures, beginning with the Romans, modified the original Greek stagecraft to suit their own situations and tastes. Yet modern scholars have carefully studied drawings on Greek vases, many of which depict actors in costume and other theater scenes. They have also sifted through literary descriptions by Greek writers and archaeological evidence from the sites of ancient theaters. Using these clues, scholars have been able to piece together what should be a reasonably accurate picture of how Greek productions were staged.

THE WORLD'S FIRST THEATER

The earliest versions of what eventually developed into theaters for play production were staging areas for religious ceremonies and celebrations. The first known example, and probably the oldest theater in the world, is in the palace at Knossus in northern Crete, the large island located southeast of the Greek mainland. This magnificent building was once the center of the main city in the empire of the Minoans, an early Greek-speaking people who inhabited Crete and many other Greek islands between 2200 and 1450 B.C. By the time of the classical Greeks, Minoan civilization had long since vanished. Yet Minoan persons and events became key elements in classical Greek mythology. And many classical Greek cultural and religious practices had their roots in Minoan times.

The theatrical area at Knossus gives evidence of one such religious practice—the use of formal dancing and singing to honor the gods. In this area, stately and colorful religious rites, very likely similar to the later dithyramb, took place. The area consists of a rectangular court, roughly 40 by 35 feet in size, and paved with large irregular stones. The court is bordered on the east and south by steps on which, scholars believe, the spectators stood and sat. Greek archaeologist Anna Michailidou gives us this description:

> At the south-east corner of the Theater, in the angle between the two banks of steps, there is a bastion-like structure which is believed to have been a sort of royal box for the king and his family. We can imagine the monarch sitting there, surrounded by as many as 500 members of his court standing on the low steps, and watching the . . . dances or religious rites.

The influence of the theatrical area at Knossus and similar areas at other Minoan palaces on later Greek theater design remains unclear. But it is likely that the basic concept of such ritual staging areas survived and became incorporated into the dithyramb in classical times. As the dithyramb evolved into formal theater in the sixth century B.C., the Greeks enlarged and modified these areas to accommodate play production.

CLASSICAL GREEK THEATERS

The first formal Greek theater was built in Athens between 550 and 534 B.C. Its exact location and physical layout are unknown, since the Athenians built over the site when larger theaters came into use a few years later. However, some evidence suggests that the first theater consisted of the same basic elements found in the Minoan versions, although considerably expanded. The rectangular court became the circular orchestra, or "dancing place," where the actors and chorus, as well as members of the dithyrambic processions, performed. And replacing the king's box was a central *thymele*, an altar for sacrificing to and honoring the gods. Surrounding much of the orchestra were wooden bleachers for the audience. The later Greek encyclopedia, the *Suidas*, reported that the bleachers collapsed in the middle of a performance, killing several spectators, about the year 499 B.C.

After this unfortunate incident, the Athenians built the Theater of Dionysus against one side of the Acropolis. In its initial form, the theater had an orchestra some eighty-five feet in diameter with a *thymele* in the center. To avoid another disaster, the seating consisted of wooden planking covering earthen tiers carved into the hillside. In a later renovation, the wooden seats were replaced by the stone versions that have endured to the present. This audience area, which could accommodate more than fourteen thousand people, became known as the *theatron*, from which the word *theater* comes. On either side of the semicircular *theatron* were the *parodoi*, entrances into the orchestra area used by actors and chorus.

Early in the fifth century B.C. the theater's designers added a structure called the *skene* in front of and facing the orchestra and *theatron*. The word *skene* originally meant "scene building" and is the source of the word "scene" so often used today in stage and film presentations. The original scene building, according to scholar James T. Allen,

> served in the first instance as a background for the actors and provided accommodations for dressing-rooms and perhaps also for the storing of various properties [stage props]. It was of a rectangular shape, sometimes with projecting wings known as *paraskenia* . . . at the sides . . . and it was seldom, if ever, more than two stories in height. Originally constructed of wood or of other perishable materials the scene-building was at first temporary in character; apparently not until the fourth century was a *skene* of stone erected.

Later, other theaters copying the Dionysus arena's design appeared across Greece. The most beautiful and best preserved is the Theater of Epidauros, located about 110 miles southwest of Athens. Built around 350 B.C. by the architect Polyclitus the Younger, the stone structure is 387 feet across; it has a top seating tier 74 feet above orchestra level and a seating capacity of fourteen thousand. The Epidauros theater remains in such good condition that the Greek National Theater and other modern dramatic companies still perform in it.

THE PERFORMERS

It was through the *parodoi* in theaters like those of Dionysus and Epidauros that the choruses marched in the opening scenes of the ancient plays. As James Butler explains:

The usual tragic and comic choruses entered singing the *par-odos* (entrance song) and led by a flute player. They were grouped in a rectangular marching formation composed of ranks and files—three by five for tragedy and four by six for comedy. Once in position in the orchestra, they turned and faced the spectators, still singing and gesturing.

During the performance that followed, the chorus members broke formation, moved from place to place, and reacted to the play's events and characters with appropriate verses and gestures. The chorus remained within the orchestra area until the finale, at which time it filed out, once more in formation and singing.

The chorus served several functions. First, it interacted with the actors, giving advice, asking questions, and expressing opinions. In Aeschylus's *The Persians*, for example, the chorus asks Persia's King Xerxes, whose armies the Greeks have defeated, "Is all your glory lost?" The king answers, "See you these poor remains of my torn robes?" "I see, I see," the chorus responds. Also, the chorus's singing and movements, which could be happy and animated or somber and morose, set the overall mood of the play and heightened the dramatic effect. In addition, says Oscar Brockett, the chorus served "an important rhythmical function, creating pauses or retardations [slowing down the action] during which the audience [could] reflect upon what had happened and what was to come."

The actors who interacted with the chorus wore elaborate masks that covered the whole head, resting on the shoulders. Made of linen stiffened with clay and brightly painted, each mask represented a stock character, such as a young maiden, a middle-aged man, an evil king, or a certain god. Writing in the second century A.D., the Greek scholar Julius Pollux listed and described many standard Greek theatrical masks. For example, for tragedy there were six for old men, eight for young men, three for male servants, and eleven for various women; and for comedy, nine for older men, eleven for younger men, seven for male servants, and seventeen for women. Special masks for gods, as well as for satyrs and other mythical creatures, were also used. Comments scholar Bernard M.W. Knox:

> The masks certainly ruled out the play of facial expression which we regard today as one of the actor's most important skills, but in the Theater of Dionysus, where even the front row of spectators was sixty feet away from the stage (the back

rows were three hundred feet away), facial expression could not have been seen anyway. And the masks had a practical value. They made it possible for the same actor to play two or even three or four different parts in different scenes of the play.

The masks also made it possible for men to play women's roles, an important and closely observed convention in ancient Greek theater. Apparently the Greeks considered it improper for women to bare their emotions, even staged ones, in public.

While the masks may have prevented the actors from utilizing facial expressions, they did not limit the use of voices. According to Oscar Brockett:

> The Greeks seem to have placed considerable emphasis upon the voice, for they judged actors above all by beauty of vocal tone and ability to adapt manner of speaking to mood and character. . . . The plays demanded three kinds of delivery: speech, recitative, and song. As the primary means of expression, the voice was trained and exercised by the actor much as it might be by an opera singer today. While the best actors attained high standards of vocal excellence, others apparently ranted and roared.

COSTUMES, PROPS, AND SCENERY

Like the masks, Greek theatrical costumes were brightly colored. This was partly to catch the eye from a distance, since most of the spectators sat so far from the actors. Another function of the bright colors was to aid in character recognition. Women's gowns, for instance, were usually of a particular color. A queen's costume was almost always purple, the traditional color of royalty, so that the spectators, who had no programs, could instantly recognize the character. Costume color also denoted mood. A character in mourning or undergoing extreme misfortune, for example, would wear black. In general, says theater historian H.C. Baldry, the actor's "own physical identity was completely concealed: mask, costume and footwear together covered him entirely except for his hands. His robe was usually ankle-length."

The actors also used props, as they do today, although the Greeks tended to use them sparingly. The most common examples were chariots, statues of gods, couches, shields and swords, and biers on which dead bodies were displayed. Special props were also associated with specific characters. Marion Geisinger states:

To differentiate among the gods and the heroes, certain easily recognizable properties were carried. Apollo [the sun god]
carried his bow, Hermes [god of invention] his magic wand,
Hercules [a heroic strongman] carried his club and lion skin,
and Perseus [a clever hero] his cap of darkness. Warriors usually appeared in full armor, with a short scarlet cloak draped
around the arm. An old man would carry a staff; a messenger
of good tidings wore a crown of olives or of laurel. A king
would carry a spear and wear a crown.

While costumes and props tended to be fairly realistic,
Greek theatrical producers left the settings largely to the audience's imagination. This was partly because the design of
the open-air theaters placed a strict limitation on the kinds
of setting a playwright could depict. In classical times, as a
rule, the action of the plays took place outdoors, in front of a
house, palace, temple, or other familiar structure. Once
added to theaters, the fixed *skene*, redecorated appropriately
by the producer, represented the fronts of these buildings.
Interiors could not be shown, and there is no solid evidence
for the existence in early Greek theaters of movable painted
scenery like that used today. However, according to tradition,
Sophocles introduced the idea of painting descriptive backgrounds on the immovable *skene*, a practice that subse-
quently became common.

SPECIAL EFFECTS

Partly to overcome the inability to show interiors, in the late
fifth century B.C. the Greeks introduced the *eccyclema*, or
"tableau machine." Violent acts such as murders were almost always committed "indoors," and therefore offstage
and out of sight, and the audience learned about them sec-
ondhand from messengers and other characters. Sometimes, however, to achieve shock value, a doorway in the
skene would open and stagehands would push out the *eccyclema*, a movable platform on rollers. On the platform,
frozen in a posed and dramatic tableau, would be usually
both murderer and victim. In the climax of productions of
Aeschylus's play, *Agamemnon*, for example, an *eccyclema*
probably displayed the body of the slain king. Standing over
Agamemnon's corpse was his wife and killer, Clytemnestra,
weapon in hand. Despite knowing full well this scene was
coming, the spectators usually gasped in horror.

The Greeks developed special theatrical effects of other
kinds to heighten the stage spectacle. Julius Pollux described

a *keraunoskopeion*, or "lightning machine," and a *bronteion*, or "thunder machine," but unfortunately he did not explain how these devices worked. Perhaps the most spectacular engine of special effects was the *machina*, from which the word "machine" is derived. As Eugene O'Neill Jr. explains, "Frequently at the close of a play the dramatist introduced a god into the action, who would naturally be expected to appear from above. He apparently was brought in by some kind of crane or derrick, called the 'machine.'" This mechanical arm probably was raised by ropes and pulleys, and the actor playing the god dangled from it on a hook.

The *machina* was also used to show spectacular human exploits, such as the hero Bellerophon riding the flying horse Pegasus. Comedy writers and producers used the *machina* in a humorous way. In Aristophanes' play *Peace*, for instance, a nonheroic farmer flew a giant dung beetle over the orchestra and *skene* and shouted, "Hi, crane-operator, take care of me!" Invariably, though, most playwrights used the device to fly in gods for the finale, an approach that eventually became overused. O'Neill comments, "The term *deus ex machina*, 'the god from the machine,' has become standard in dramatic criticism. It . . . refers to awkward, mechanical, and unconvincing means which a playwright is forced to employ if he cannot work out a satisfactory resolution to his plot."

CAUGHT UP IN THE EXCITEMENT

All these theatrical elements—masks, costumes, machines, and the like—were designed to entertain the audience. The playwrights and producers demonstrably attained this goal, for the theater was immensely popular in Greece. In Athens in the fifth century B.C., for example, performances were always sold out. The Athenians, it seems, also invented the theater ticket. This was necessary because nearly all the city's two hundred thousand or more people desired entrance into a building that seated no more than seventeen thousand at its largest expansion. Yet playgoing was not exclusively a pastime of the well-to-do. About the year 450 B.C., the democratic leader Pericles instituted a special government fund to provide tickets for the poor.

Greek theater audiences differed from modern ones mainly in their outward show of enthusiasm. As James H. Butler puts it:

If it were possible to project ourselves back in time, to attend a series of performances at one of the great festivals given in the Theater of Dionysus, the strongest impressions we would have, aside from those caused by strange scenic and acting conventions, would be of the audience. For they were caught up in a feverish excitement, an intense interest in the outcome of the various contests. Their volatility and enthusiasm were more characteristic of present-day football and baseball spectators than of the quiet... often passive demeanor exhibited by our theater audiences. The hundreds directly competing for prizes and honors in the City Dionysia sharpened the appetite for victory. Add to this group several hundred, perhaps several thousand, former chorus members, dithyrambic performers, flute players, and extras sprinkled among the audience. They had competed in previous festivals and were quite knowledgeable on the finer points and techniques of performance. Refreshments to sustain the "dawn to dusk" audience were hawked [sold by roving vendors], thereby increasing the general noise and commotion.

Greek audiences differed from today's in another way. Because the Greeks invented the theater, their audiences witnessed something unique, an institution that existed nowhere else and developed and evolved before their eyes. Theatrical conventions and ideas that today seem run-of-the-mill were, in ancient Athens, fresh and exciting. It was in this stimulating, creative atmosphere that some of the greatest playwrights of all time, including Sophocles, worked their magic.

Chronology

B.C.

534

The theatrical innovator Thespis, credited as the world's first actor, wins the first prize at Athens's City Dionysia dramatics competition.

CA. 496

Sophocles is born at Colonus, near Athens.

468

Sophocles wins his first top prize at the great Dionysia for the play *Triptolemus*, beating Aeschylus, the greatest dramatist of the time.

CA. 447

Sophocles writes and produces *Ajax*.

443

The great statesman Pericles appoints Sophocles treasurer of the federated city-states making up Athens's empire.

441

Sophocles writes and produces *Antigone*.

440

Sophocles is elected one of Athens's ten generals and, along with Pericles, lays siege to the rebel city-state of Samos.

CA. 429

Sophocles writes and produces *Oedipus the King*, which later generations will judge his masterpiece.

CA. 428

Sophocles writes and produces *The Women of Trachis*.

CA. 420

Sophocles' friend, the historian Herodotus, who will later be called the father of history, dies.

CA. 415

Sophocles possibly elected to a second generalship; he writes and produces *Electra.*

409

Sophocles writes and produces *Philoctetes.*

406

The playwright Euripides, Sophocles' colleague and friend, dies; Sophocles writes *Oedipus at Colonus*; Sophocles dies.

405

Tributes to Sophocles appear in the lines of the comic plays *Frogs*, by Aristophanes, and *Muses*, by Phrynichus.

CA. 335–322

The Greek philosopher-scholar Aristotle writes the *Poetics*, in which he praises Sophocles' writing skill and cites *Oedipus the King* as a model for great tragedy.

A.D.

1585

The first modern production of Sophocles' *Oedipus the King* is staged in Italy, after which hundreds of versions of this and other plays by Sophocles are produced in each succeeding century.

1907

A papyrus containing about four hundred lines of Sophocles' satyr play *Ichneutae* is discovered.

1913

Famed psychoanalyst Sigmund Freud publishes *Totem and Taboo*, in which he details the "Oedipus complex," a theory of human sexual desires based on the relationships in Sophocles' *Oedipus the King.*

1944

Stage and film star Laurence Olivier plays Oedipus at London's New Theater in one of the twentieth century's most memorable interpretations of Sophocles' immortal character.

1967

Actor Christopher Plummer portrays Oedipus in a film version of *Oedipus the King.*

THE SURVIVING
PLAYS OF SOPHOCLES

TITLE	MAIN CHARACTERS	DATE WRITTEN
Ajax	Ajax, Odysseus, Teucer, and the goddess Athena	ca. 447 B.C.
Antigone	Antigone, Ismene, Creon, and Haemon	441 B.C.
Oedipus the King	Oedipus, Jocasta, Creon, and Tiresias	ca. 429 B.C.
The Women of Trachis	Heracles, Deianira, Hyllus, and Lichas	ca. 428 B.C.
Electra	Orestes, Clytemnestra, Electra, Chrysothemis, and Aegisthus	ca. 415 B.C.
Philoctetes	Philoctetes, Odysseus, Neoptolemus, and the god Heracles	409 B.C.
Oedipus at Colonus	Oedipus, Antigone, Ismene, Creon, Theseus, and Polynices	406 B.C.

FOR FURTHER RESEARCH

ABOUT SOPHOCLES AND HIS WORKS

Aristotle, *Poetics*, in Robert Maynard Hutchins, ed., *The Works of Aristotle*, vol. 9 of Great Books of the Western World. Chicago: Encyclopedia Britannica, 1952.

William N. Bates, *Sophocles: Poet and Dramatist.* New York: Russell & Russell, 1969.

Michael Grant, *The Classical Greeks.* New York: Charles Scribner's Sons, 1989.

Richard C. Jebb, trans., *The Complete Plays of Sophocles.* New York: Bantam Books, 1967.

Charles Segal, *Oedipus Tyrannus: Tragic Heroism and the Limits of Knowledge.* New York: Twayne Publishers, 1993.

Sophocles, *Complete Works.* 2 vols. Trans. F. Storr. Cambridge, MA: Harvard University Press, 1967.

Sophocles, *Oedipus the King*, trans. Bernard M.W. Knox. New York: Pocket Books, 1959.

Sophocles, *Oedipus the King and Oedipus at Colonus*, trans. Charles R. Walker. New York: Doubleday, 1966.

Thomas Woodward, ed., *Sophocles: A Collection of Critical Essays.* Englewood Cliffs, NJ: Prentice-Hall, 1966.

ABOUT ANCIENT GREEK THEATER, MYTHS, AND SOCIETY

James T. Allen, *Stage Antiquities of the Greeks and Romans and Their Influence.* New York: Cooper Square Publishers, 1963.

Isaac Asimov, *The Greeks: A Great Adventure.* Boston: Houghton Mifflin, 1965.

H.C. Baldry, *The Greek Tragic Theater.* New York: W.W. Norton, 1971.

David Bellingham, *An Introduction to Greek Mythology.* Secaucus, NJ: Chartwell Books, 1989.

Sue Blundell, *Women in Ancient Greece.* Cambridge, MA: Harvard University Press, 1995.

Oscar G. Brockett, *History of the Theater.* Boston: Allyn & Bacon, 1982.

James H. Butler, *The Theater and Drama of Greece and Rome.* San Francisco: Chandler Publishing, 1972.

Lionel Casson, *Masters of Ancient Comedy.* New York: Macmillan, 1960.

Sheldon Cheney, *The Theater: Three Thousand Years of Drama, Acting, and Stagecraft.* New York: Tudor Publishing, 1939.

Edmund Fuller, *A Pageant of the Theater.* New York: Thomas Y. Crowell, 1965.

Marion Geisinger, *Plays, Players, and Playwrights: An Illustrated History of the Theater.* New York: Hart Publishing, 1971.

Moses Hadas, ed., *The Complete Plays of Aristophanes.* New York: Bantam Books, 1962.

Phyllis Hartnoll, *The Concise History of the Theater.* New York: Harry N. Abrams, 1968.

Rhoda A. Hendricks, trans., *Classical Gods and Heroes.* New York: Morrow Quill, 1974.

Herodotus, *Histories,* trans. Aubrey de Selincourt. New York: Penguin Books, 1972.

Homer, the *Odyssey,* retold by Barbara L. Picard. New York: Oxford University Press, 1952.

———, the *Iliad,* retold by Barbara L. Picard. New York: Oxford University Press, 1960.

Anna Michailidou, *Knossus: A Complete Guide to the Palace of Minos.* Athens: Ekdotike Athenon, 1993.

Don Nardo, *Ancient Greece.* San Diego: Lucent Books, 1994.

———, *Greek and Roman Theater.* San Diego: Lucent Books, 1995.

———, *Life in Ancient Greece.* San Diego: Lucent Books, 1996.

———, *The Age of Pericles.* San Diego: Lucent Books, 1996.

Robert Payne, *Ancient Greece: The Triumph of a Culture.* New York: W.W. Norton, 1964.

Arthur Pickard-Cambridge, *The Dramatic Festivals of Athens.* Oxford: Oxford University Press, 1968.

C.A. Robinson, ed., *An Anthology of Greek Drama.* New York: Holt, Rinehart, and Winston, 1960.

Paul Roche, trans., *The Orestes Plays of Aeschylus.* New York: New American Library, 1962.

Ian Scott-Kilvert, trans., *The Rise and Fall of Athens: Nine Greek Lives by Plutarch.* New York: Penguin Books, 1960.

Immanuel Velikovsky, *Oedipus and Akhnaton: Myth and History.* New York: Doubleday, 1960.

Michael Wood, *In Search of the Trojan War.* New York: New American Library, 1985.

INDEX